Engaged Clinical Practice

Engaged Clinical Practice

Preparing Mentor Teachers and University-Based Educators to Support Teacher Candidate Learning and Development

Edited by
Philip E. Bernhardt, Thomas R. Conway,
and Greer M. Richardson

ROWMAN & LITTLEFIELD
Lanham • Boulder • New York • London

Published by Rowman & Littlefield
An imprint of The Rowman & Littlefield Publishing Group, Inc.
4501 Forbes Boulevard, Suite 200, Lanham, Maryland 20706
www.rowman.com

6 Tinworth Street, London SE11 5AL, United Kingdom

Copyright © 2021 by Philip E. Bernhardt, Thomas R. Conway, Greer M. Richardson

All rights reserved. No part of this book may be reproduced in any form or by any electronic or mechanical means, including information storage and retrieval systems, without written permission from the publisher, except by a reviewer who may quote passages in a review.

British Library Cataloguing in Publication Information Available

Library of Congress Cataloging-in-Publication Data

Names: Bernhardt, Philip E., 1977- editor.
Title: Engaged clinical practice : preparing mentor teachers and university-based educators to support teacher candidate learning / edited by Philip E. Bernhardt, Thomas R. Conway, and Greer M. Richardson.
Description: Lanham : Rowman & Littlefield, [2020] | Includes bibliographical references. | Summary: "The primary purpose of this text is to provide readers a varied set of examples from teacher preparation programs that have established effective systems, practices, and/or pedagogies"—Provided by publisher.
Identifiers: LCCN 2020018611 (print) | LCCN 2020018612 (ebook) | ISBN 9781475849905 (cloth) | ISBN 9781475849912 (paperback) | ISBN 9781475849929 (epub)
Subjects: LCSH: Teachers—Training of. | Mentoring in education.
Classification: LCC LB1707 .E64 2020 (print) | LCC LB1707 (ebook) | DDC 370.71/1—dc23
LC record available at https://lccn.loc.gov/2020018611
LC ebook record available at https://lccn.loc.gov/2020018612

Contents

	Foreword	vii
	Acknowledgments	xi
Introduction		1
Chapter 1	Supporting the Development of Specialized Content Knowledge for Teaching Music, Physical Education, and Other "Specials" *Ian Parker Renga, George Kamberelis, Alissa Tower, Cori Woytek, and Caroline Powders-Forrest*	7
Chapter 2	Improving Educator Preparation Using Asynchronous, Online Professional Development *Allison R. Magagnosc and Ingrid T. Everett*	21
Chapter 3	A Model of Collaboration: Mentor Teachers, Teacher Candidates, and University-Based Teacher Educators *Deborah Yost, Greer M. Richardson, Thomas R. Conway, Allison R. Magagnosc, and Alana M. Mellor*	33
Chapter 4	Enhancing Mentor Teachers' Experience, Effectiveness, and Engagement Through Professional Development and University Communication *Glenda L. Black and Anna-Liisa Mottonen*	49

Chapter 5	Mentor Study Groups as Sites for Mentor Teacher Learning *Amy R. Guenther, Lindsay J. Wexler, Susan K. Brondyk, Randi N. Stanulis, and Stacey Pylman*	65
Chapter 6	Cultivating Clinical Coaching through Collaboration at Wright State University *Romena M. Garrett Holbert, Amy E. Elston, and Tracey A. Kramer*	79
Chapter 7	Using an Online Platform to Prepare Mentor Teachers as Clinical Coaches *Brooke K. Langan and Kathleen L. Post*	93
Chapter 8	Practice-Based Coaching to Impact Early Childhood Teacher Candidate Uptake of Evidence-Based Practice in Clinical Internship *Toni Miguel*	105
Chapter 9	Only the Best: Ensuring High-Quality Mentors for Teacher Candidates *Amy Rogers, Gwyneth Price, and John Ziegler*	117
Chapter 10	Developing Teacher Candidates for the 21st Century: Engaging the Village *Dianne M. Gut-Zippert, Pamela C. Beam, Heidi Mullins, and Kathleen Haskell*	131
	About the Editors	143
	About the Contributors	145

Foreword

From 2018 to 2019, I was fortunate to be elected president of the Association of Teacher Educators (ATE). The vision and theme of my presidency focused on clinical practice within the context of preparing our future teachers. Part of the opportunity I was given in this leadership role was to form a task force that would carry on the theme of my conference. Thus, the Task Force on Addressing the Needs of Cooperating/Mentor/Associate Teachers in their Practices and Roles as Mentors and Supervisors of the Novice Teacher was launched with the appointments of co-chairs Dr. Philip Bernhardt; Dr. Thomas Conway, Cabrini University; and Dr. Greer Richardson.

This book is one of the key initiatives of this task force. In this foreword, I explain the catalyst for the book and the background for this initiative that in some ways is nothing short of serendipitous but also has strong grounding in the influence and impact of the ATE professional community. As a career-long teacher educator, I have advocated for attending to the needs of the school-based teacher educator and adjunct supervisor. They are the forgotten group in the funding equations of policy makers who do not consider the value of supporting and resourcing the professional development needs of a teacher educator. How did I evolve this passion?

As a doctoral student, I was fortunate to be situated as a graduate assistant in the Office of Laboratory Experiences at the University of Maryland, College Park. There, I assisted the director, Dr. James Greenberg, in managing the five teacher education centers that were part of the mutually funded teacher preparation partnerships with the area school systems.

Coming into doctoral studies as a former elementary teacher, my world expanded into teacher education, and, there, a new identity and passion were formed. I was mentored by a cadre of stellar teacher center coordinators and my director, who consistently engaged in inquiry about their practices, shared their research, and modeled new pedagogies associated with their practices. They were practitioner–scholars before the term was popular as it is today.

My doctoral studies led me to understand in deeper ways the many dilemmas and ethical issues associated with the teacher educator's boundary-spanning roles and how the needs of the cooperating/mentor teacher needed to be addressed in equal proportion to the teacher candidate. Upon finishing my doctorate, I went on to George Washington University to assume the role of director of the GWU Office of Laboratory Experiences.

There, I continued to develop, with colleagues, a course in supervision and mentoring for our doctoral students, who were the ones often assigned to cover field supervision in our teacher preparation programs. One of my students was Philip Bernhardt, who took the reins in advocating for better resources and professional development for the cooperating/mentor teacher. His inquiry for my course involved developing an academy for cooperating/mentor teachers with his peer, Dr. Vince O'Neill, and later, as he moved into academe, he continued this work at the Metropolitan State University of Denver.

We have remained connected through ATE, and now, with the opportunity to create a task force, Philip was my first choice in exploring how we could put this initiative together. Dr. Bernhardt was already well on the way to developing the vision for this book, which became integrated into the task force initiative and pulled in more like-minded colleagues in Tom Conway and Greer Richardson, both stellar practitioner–scholars in teacher education.

I have observed a consistent theme in policy reports and standards on teacher preparation (AACTE, 2018; AASCU, 2017; ATE, 2016, 2018; CAEP, 2019; CCSSO, 2012; Flessner & Lecklider, 2017; NCATE, 2010) that calls for renewed emphasis on the clinical practice components of teacher preparation programs that need stronger connections between theory and practice as well as attention to teacher educator pedagogical practices (i.e., *approximations of practice*; Grossman, 2010) that provides mediated opportunities for the novice teacher to apply their knowledge, skills, and dispositions toward their professional roles in real school contexts.

ATE has a long-standing history in developing the preservice field-experience standards and teacher educator standards (ATE, 2016, 2018) and attracting and developing programs and initiatives focused on supporting the teacher educator's work and scholarship. In fact, ATE was originally founded in 1920 as the National Association of Directors of Supervised Student Teaching (Flessner & Lecklider, 2017).

As ATE's scope and reach has expanded to encompass both school- and university-based professionals who prepare and develop teachers, limited attention has been paid to the needs of the cooperating/mentor/associate teacher. In particular, attention is needed in preparing them to effectively enact their essential roles in supervision and mentoring.

It is most gratifying to see an ATE scholarly product dedicated to addressing the needs of the school-based cooperating/mentor teacher and the adjunct university supervisor. These individuals play an essential role in teacher preparation and assure the growth and development of our future teachers. However, in many programs' designs, they are loosely connected to the faculty who teach the curriculum.

The work they do constitutes the intangibles, the unexplained recurring phenomena attributed to bridging the complexities associated with (a) different personalities and orientations toward teaching practice; (b) mediating the different situations that arise between needs of teacher candidates and cooperating/mentor teachers to assure a continued productive partnership; and, most importantly, (c) negotiating productive experiences for all the participants involved.

Through critical conversations of objective observational data aligned to frameworks for effective teaching, teacher educators navigate, negotiate, mentor, direct, coach, assess, and evaluate and provide many types of resources and emotional support as needed for teacher candidate growth. The role of the teacher educator in the clinical realm of teacher preparation represents nuanced practices that can make or break the motivational state of a preservice teacher and can impact their successful completion of requirements for teacher licensure.

This publication provides a window into the practices that sit in the "third space" (Cuenca et al., 2011) of teacher preparation and the foundational relationship-building processes that lead to trust and establishment of productive relationships for those involved.

I applaud the teacher educator practitioner–scholars who have contributed to this work. They are the new leaders in this line of inquiry. My hope is that the reader will find inspiration, ideas, and models to build on in their own contexts as well as new knowledge and understandings that will assist them in their continuous improvement efforts associated with exemplary clinical preparation of preservice teachers.

Patricia Sari Tate, PhD
George Washington University
ATE President 2018–2019

References

American Association of Colleges for Teacher Education (AACTE). (2018). *A pivot toward clinical practice, its lexicon, and the renewal of educator preparation*. Washington, DC: Author.

American Association of State Colleges and Universities (AASCU). (2017). *Preparing teachers in today's challenging context: Key issues, policy directions, and implications for leaders of AASCU universities*. Washington, DC: Author.

Association of Teacher Educators (ATE). (2018). *ATE standards for teacher educators*. Manassas, VA: Author.

Association of Teacher Educators (ATE). (2016). *ATE standards for field experiences in teacher education*. Manassas, VA: Author.

Council of Chief State School Officers (CCSSO). (2012). *Our responsibility, our promise: Transforming educator preparation and entry into the profession*. Washington, DC: Author.

Cuenca, A., Schmeichel, M., Butler, B., Dinkelman, T., & Nichols, J. R. (2011). Creating a "third space" in student teaching: Implications for the university supervisor's status as outsider. *Teaching and Teacher Education, 27*, 1068–1077.

Flessner, R., & Lecklider, D. R. (Eds.). (2017). *The power of clinical preparation in teacher education*. New York: Rowman & Littlefield.

Grossman, P. (2010, May). Learning to practice: The design of clinical experiences in teacher preparation [Policy brief]. Washington, DC: National Education Association.

National Council for Accreditation of Teacher Education (NCATE). (2010). *Transforming teacher education through clinical practice: A national strategy to prepare effective teachers*. Washington, DC: Author.

Acknowledgments

We would like to fondly thank Patricia Sari Tate, PhD, and past president (2018–2019) of the Association of Teacher Educators (ATE), for supporting, encouraging, and helping to vision this edited text. Pat also invited us to lead an ATE Task Force focusing on supporting the needs of mentor teachers and university-based educators; the text is a product of this work. Dr. Tate is a leader in the field, and this book is a tribute to her tireless work to influence and advance teacher preparation in meaningful and significant ways. We are thankful for her guidance, kindness, and gracious wisdom.

We would also like to acknowledge a number of individuals supporting this project as guest editors. As experts in mentoring and clinical experiences, each of these individuals contributed powerful insights across the various chapters. A special note of gratitude goes to Thomas Sutton, Amy Rogers, Karen Dunlap, Patricia Tate, Rubén Garza, Romena Holbert, Vince O'Neill, and Sheila Conway.

This text is a compilation of ten unique projects representing a diverse set of teacher preparation programs. Each chapter tells a story of transformation, development, and renewal. We want to thank all the authors for the work they are currently engaged in to improve mentoring practices, clinical experiences, and the overall educational experiences for their teacher candidates. Providing a forum for teacher educators to share their stories has been a tremendous learning experience, and we feel grateful for this opportunity. We hope you find the projects both instructive and inspiring as you consider how to enhance and develop your own preparation program.

Finally, we want to acknowledge that projects such as these are possible only through the support and encouragement of our families. A huge thank-you to Ellen, Emma, and Oliver Bernhardt; Brian and Parker Wilson; and Thoth Weeda for supporting each of us as we spent time putting this text together.

Introduction

Clinical experiences, supported by well-prepared mentor teachers and university-based teacher educators, are essential for developing successful teacher candidates. While the design, structure, expectations, curricula, and length of these significant learning opportunities often vary among preparation programs, a common feature is that teacher candidates work in partnered educational settings engaged in teaching that is closely aligned with coursework and in collaboration with individuals tasked with supporting their growth, development, and entry into the profession (AACTE, 2018).

There is an extensive body of research supporting the assertion that mentor teachers and university-based educators who are professionally prepared with the requisite skills, knowledge, understandings, and dispositions are a cornerstone of clinical practice (AACTE, 2018; Darling-Hammond, 2014; Flessner & Lecklider, 2017a, 2017b; Grossman et al., 2009; Hammerness et al., 2005; Hollins, 2015). That said, many preparation programs lack systematic approaches and strategies for preparing mentors and university-based educators for the important task of coaching, supervising, and evaluating teacher candidates during the clinical portions of their program (Aspfors & Fransson, 2015; Izadinia, 2015; Sayeski & Paulsen, 2012; Smith & Avetisian, 2011). As a result, these practitioners do not always receive the necessary development and support to be effective in their role.

There is clear consensus within the field that clinical practice, supported by well-prepared and supported mentor teachers and university-based educators, is critical for the successful preparation of teacher candidates (AACTE,

2013, 2018; Clarke et al., 2014; Darling-Hammond, 2000; NCATE, 2010; NCTQ, 2011). Whether candidates are enrolled in a traditional undergraduate or graduate preparation program or a residency-based pathway or are seeking one of the numerous alternative routes to licensure, it is essential to match them with experienced and prepared professionals who understand how to support their cognitive, emotional, and pedagogical development.

This thoughtful pairing is essential because teacher candidates tend to view their field-based experiences as the most significant component of the preparation process and perceive their mentor teachers as essential to their success (Clarke et al., 2014; Kirk et al., 2006; Weiss & Weiss, 2001). Nonetheless, within many educator programs, the current practices for preparing mentor teachers and university-based educators to be effective clinical coaches are often inadequate and fail to fully address their roles, responsibilities, and expectations (Clarke et al., 2014). Unfortunately, this highly impactful element of the educator preparation process just does not typically garner the time, focus, or necessary resources that it deserves.

This gap in preparation is critical to examine, especially when contextualized with research documenting that those involved in consistent and intentional professional development related to mentoring and coaching are more likely than their untrained counterparts to provide evaluative and rather judgmental feedback, interact more when planning lessons and developing assessments, create a reflective environment to discuss teaching practices, and utilize the clinical supervision model (Bryant & Currin, 1995; Kent, 2001; Killian & McIntyre, 1987; Koster et al., 1998).

Similarly, Gareis and Grant (2012) found that training mentor-teachers is associated with stronger student teacher performance as well as more effective assessment and feedback practices. Weiss and Weiss (2001) have suggested there is wide acceptance of the idea that mentor-teachers "are the most powerful influence on the quality of student teaching experience and often shape what student teachers learn by the way they mentor" (p. 134). Mentor teachers and university-based educators need to be intentionally, consistently, and thoughtfully prepared to support teacher candidates.

In recent years the National Council for the Accreditation of Teacher Education (NCATE, 2010), Association of Teacher Educators (ATE, 2016), and the American Association of Colleges for Teacher Education (AACTE, 2018) have called for teacher preparation programs to situate clinical practice at the center of curricula. While there is certainly guidance in the literature highlighting instructive approaches for preparing and supporting mentor teachers and university-based educators, there is tremendous value in listening to and learning from preparation programs that are systematically and successfully engaged in this work and positively impacting teacher candidates.

This clinical work is essential for effective teacher preparation, as it provides context for teacher candidates to practice the pedagogical work of teaching in authentic educational settings with the support and guidance of mentors as well as develop and hone their craft as they receive consistent support and feedback (Alter & Coggshall, 2009; Grossman, 2010; Guha et al., 2016). However, for this to happen, there is a need to more deeply understand how to effectively prepare mentor teachers and university-based educators to support teacher candidate learning. This edited text shares evidence of innovations and developments within 10 teacher preparation programs whose faculty and leadership are committed to this critical clinical work.

In the publication *A Pivot toward Clinical Practice, Its Lexicon, and the Renewal of Educator Preparation*, the AACTE Clinical Practice Commission (2018) offered 10 proclamations for effective clinical practice. In particular, the mutual benefit proclamation posits that school- and university-based educators are essential to the success of teacher candidates, as they "play necessary, vital and synergistic roles in clinical preparation programs" (p. 33). When conceptualizing and writing the chapters included in this text, authors considered two questions directly connected to this proclamation:

1. How do teacher preparation programs develop mentor teachers and university-based educators as effective clinical coaches?
2. How do teacher preparation programs work in collaboration with schools to support teacher-candidates during clinical internship?

The primary purpose of the chapters included in this edited text are to provide readers a varied set of examples from teacher preparation programs that have established effective systems, practices, and pedagogies to develop and support mentor teachers and university-based educators in becoming effective clinical coaches. With an eye toward replication, this text offers readers detailed and nuanced perspectives of successful programs. The text endeavors to shine a bright light on those programmatic efforts shaping teacher preparation in impactful, meaningful, and sustainable ways. This text will be of primary interest to all those working in organizations, institutes of higher education, alternative licensure programs, and schools and districts involved with the preparation of teacher candidates.

As you read the text, we encourage you to consider selected terms and definitions from the AACTE Clinical Practice Commission's *Lexicon of Practice* (2018). We made an intentional decision to adopt these terms as part of the text and asked contributing authors to utilize them within their chapters. The terms and definitions are included here as a reference for readers.

1. *Clinical practice:* Teacher candidates work in partnered educational settings engaged in teaching that is closely integrated into coursework.
2. *Clinical coaching:* The practices in which school and university teacher educators engage, including supervision and mentoring.
3. *Clinical internship:* The clinical experience in which the teacher candidates assume full responsibility for pedagogy and are mentored/coached by school and university teacher educators.
4. *Mentor teacher:* The school-based teacher educator paired with the teacher candidate.
5. *Teacher candidate:* Those enrolled in teacher preparation programs.
6. *Teacher preparation:* The work done to prepare teacher candidates for entry into the profession.
7. *School-based teacher educator:* Assumes responsibilities for mentoring and partnership and has the school as his or her institutional home.
8. *University-based teacher educator:* Assumes responsibilities of evaluation, coaching, instruction, and partnership and has the university as his or her institutional home.

References

Alter, J., & Coggshall, J. G. (2009, March). *Teaching as a clinical practice profession: Implications for teacher preparation and state policy* [Issue brief]. ERIC. https://files.eric.ed.gov/fulltext/ED543819.pdf

American Association of Colleges for Teacher Education (AACTE). (2013). *The clinical preparation of teachers: A policy brief.* Washington, DC: Author.

American Association of Colleges for Teacher Education (AACTE). (2018). *A pivot toward clinical practice, its lexicon, and the renewal of educator preparation.* http://www.nysed.gov/common/nysed/files/cpc-aactecpcreport.pdf

Aspfors, J., & Fransson, G. (2015). Research on mentor education for mentors of newly qualified teachers: A qualitative meta-synthesis. *Teaching and Teacher Education, 48,* 75–86.

Association of Teacher Educators (ATE). (2016). *Standards for field experiences in teacher education.* Fairfax, VA: Author.

Bryant, M., & Currin, D. (1995). Views of teacher evaluation from novice and expert evaluators. *Journal of Curriculum and Supervision, 10,* 250–261.

Clarke, A., Triggs, V., & Nielsen, W. (2014). CTs participation in teacher education: A review of the literature. *Review of Educational Research, 84*(2), 162–202.

Darling-Hammond, L. (2000). How teacher education matters. *Journal of Teacher Education, 51*(3), 166–173.

Darling-Hammond, L. (2014). Strengthening clinical preparation: The Holy Grail of teacher education. *Peabody Journal of Education, 89*(4), 547–561.

Flessner, R., & Lecklider, D. (2017a). *The power of clinical preparation in teacher education: Embedding teacher preparation within P–12 school contexts.* Lanham, MD: Rowman & Littlefield.

Flessner, R., & Lecklider, D. (2017b). *Case studies of clinical preparation in teacher education: An examination of three teacher preparation partnerships.* Lanham, MD: Rowman & Littlefield.

Gareis, C. R., & Grant, L. W. (2012). Investigating student teacher outcomes of a clinical faculty program. *The Teacher Educators' Journal, 19,* 43–70.

Grossman, P. (2010). *Learning to practice: The design of clinical experience in teacher preparation.* [Policy brief]. Washington, DC: American Association of Colleges for Teacher Education and National Education Association.

Grossman, P., Hammerness, K., & McDonald, M. (2009). Redefining teaching, re-imagining teacher education. *Teachers and Teaching: Theory and Practice, 15*(2), 273–289.

Guha, R., Hyler, M. E., & Darling-Hammond, L. (2016). *The teacher residency: An innovative model for preparing teachers.* Washington, DC: The Learning Policy Institute.

Hammerness, K., Darling-Hammond, L., Grossman, P., Rust, F., & Shulman, L. (2005). The design of teacher education programs. In L. Darling-Hammond & J. Bransford (Eds.), *Preparing teachers for a changing world: What teachers should learn and be able to do* (pp. 390–441). San Francisco: Jossey-Bass.

Hollins, E. R. (2015). *Rethinking field experiences in preservice teacher preparation: Meeting new challenges for accountability.* New York: Routledge.

Izadinia, M. (2015). A closer look at the role of mentor teachers in shaping preservice teachers' professional identity. *Teaching and Teacher Education, 52,* 1–10.

Kent, S. I. (2001). Supervision of student teachers: Practices of CTs prepared in a clinical supervision course. *Journal of Curriculum and Supervision, 16*(3), 228–244.

Killian, J., & McIntyre, D. J. (1987). The influence of supervisory training for cooperating teachers on preservice teachers' development during early field experiences. *Journal of Educational Research, 80*(5), 277–282.

Kirk, D., Macdonald, D., & O'Sullivan, M. (2006). *The handbook of physical education.* London: Sage.

Koster, B., Korthagen, F. A. J., & Wubbels, T. (1998). Is there anything left for us? Functions of CTs and teacher educators. *European Journal of Teacher Education, 21*(1), 75–87.

National Council for the Accreditation of Teacher Education (NCATE). (2010). *Transforming teacher education through clinical practice: A national strategy to prepare effective teachers.* Washington, DC: Author.

National Council on Teacher Quality. (2011). *Student teaching in the United States*. Washington, DC: Author.

Sayeski, K. L., & Paulsen, K. J. (2012). Student teacher evaluations of cooperating teachers as indices of effective mentoring. *Teacher Education Quarterly, 39*(2), 117–130.

Smith, E. R., & Avetisian, V. (2011). Learning to teach with two mentors: Revisiting the "two-worlds pitfall" in student teaching. *The Teacher Educator, 46*(4), 335–354.

Weiss, E. M., & Weiss, S. (2001). Doing reflective supervision with student teachers in a professional development school culture. *Reflective Practice, 2,* 125–154.

CHAPTER ONE

Supporting the Development of Specialized Content Knowledge for Teaching Music, Physical Education, and Other "Specials"

Ian Parker Renga, George Kamberelis, Alissa Tower, Cori Woytek, and Caroline Powders-Forrest

A common refrain voiced by teacher candidates pursuing licensure in what some school districts refer to as "specials" subjects—art, music, physical education, and even business or computer programming—is that things look different in their classrooms than in literacy, math, science, and social studies classrooms. These candidates note how students often come to class craving opportunities for creative expression or to blow off steam and thus warrant unorthodox instructional strategies. Also, many of their students are already accomplished artists, musicians, or athletes due to extracurricular enrichment, while others are complete novices.

The wide range of experience, ability, and exposure to the content can complicate lesson planning. Amplifying this concern is the fact that, unlike their elementary or secondary peers, many specials candidates are licensed to teach across the K–12 spectrum and must therefore be masterful at differentiating their content for younger and older students. Many of these teacher candidates also work in multiple schools, as districts allocate limited resources to boost instruction in high-stakes content areas, such as math and literacy (Graham et al., 2002; McNeil, 2000; West, 2012).

Addressing these needs requires something more (Ward et al., 2015), including class assignments that match the specials classroom and insights from, as one candidate put it in her feedback on the authors' licensure program, "a PE [sic] point of view that not all observers understand." This issue is not unique to specials. Navigating the tension between pedagogical and content concerns remains an enduring challenge within teacher communities

(Grossman et al., 2001). Indeed, teacher educators are still wrestling with Shulman's (1987) call for a more nuanced understanding of the pedagogical content knowledge necessary for excellent teaching.

Ball et al. (2008) have carefully mapped the content area–specific knowledge teachers must draw upon as well as its intersection with curricular and pedagogical content knowledge (see also Berry et al., 2015). The focus becomes how good teachers possess *specialized content knowledge* of their subject that is uniquely applicable to teaching. Such teachers are more adept at unpacking ideas and procedures to make "features of particular content visible and learnable by students" (Ball et al., 2008, p. 400).

Comparisons between disciplinary experts and teachers are instructive here. Mathematicians do not need to understand, as math teachers do, how fractional thinking develops or how culturally informed experiences, manipulatives, and social interaction can be leveraged to facilitate, for example, algebraic thinking. Similarly, artists can expertly ply their craft without knowing, as art teachers must, how to guide diverse learners in tasks such as mixing paint, spinning pots, or making sophisticated marks on vellum.

Musicians only need routines of practice, but music teachers must know how to establish such routines with novices. Athletes can likewise excel without knowledge of best practices for nurturing fitness and health resiliency; yet this knowledge is crucial for successful physical educators. So, while professional teaching standards emphasize practices such as student-centered instruction and responsive classroom management, what these practices look like in the art studio, music room, or school gymnasium requires elaboration for prospective teachers.

In this chapter, the authors explore how specialized content knowledge (SCK) for specials teacher candidates in two subjects (music and physical education) emerged and was addressed by teacher educators within a clinical residency program. The following research questions guided the study: Where is SCK visible in the candidates' clinical experiences within the program? How do programmatic expectations, tools, and curricula support or constrain SCK learning? What modifications can university-based teacher educators make to support teacher candidates pursuing licensure in "specials" subjects?

Methods

Setting and Participants

The study took place in a yearlong teacher residency program, within which the authors serve as faculty and administrators. Teacher candidates in the program start by attending an intensive summer orientation on campus.

They then take asynchronous online courses while practicing their craft daily in K–12 classrooms under the guidance of a mentor teacher, who provides feedback on the candidate's progress.

Placed in schools mostly around the state of Colorado, candidates are monitored by a support team that includes their mentor teacher along with a boundary-spanning teacher educator, referred to as a regional coordinator, who is typically a retired or veteran educator living near the host school. Candidates are also supported by a university-based teacher educator, or clinical coach, who teaches courses and tracks the progress of a group of candidates. Reflection for growth is fostered through multiple formal observations of teaching, including virtual observations facilitated through Edthena, an online platform for video-based clinical coaching.

For clinical coaches, the videos afford a valuable window into both the novices' teaching and their developing instructional knowledge. Each of the clinical coaches—all experienced former teachers—are pedagogical generalists tasked with coordinating standards, content knowledge expectations, and the specialized expertise of mentor teachers and regional coordinators. Two candidates in the teacher education program consented to participate in the study: Kathleen (pseudonyms used for both participants), who was pursuing a license to teach physical education, and Joy, who was seeking a license to teach music.

Data and Analysis Strategies

Data included the teacher candidates' lesson plans, progress evaluation forms, responses to a program satisfaction survey, and annotated Edthena videos of their teaching. To address the research questions, a research team, comprising the five chapter authors, engaged in a form of collaborative action research emphasizing inquiry for understanding (Cochran-Smith & Lytle, 2009). Specifically, the team undertook a qualitative, comparative case study (Stake, 1995, 2005) of the two teacher candidates, Kathleen and Joy.

Data analysis began with the research team breaking into two groups, each of which met to review the data collaboratively for one of the two candidates through the SCK lens. The whole team then came together to compare notes and get a sense of emerging issues and themes. From there, the team probed deeper into the data, refining preliminary themes in a way that disclosed a fundamental tension in teaching—a tension foregrounded by SCK—between navigating one's disciplinary knowledge and the demands of classroom teaching (Grossman et al., 2001).

Analyses yielded several insights into the possibilities and challenges of developing candidates' SCK for their respective subjects, as well as insights about how university-based teacher educators might support specials candidates to understand and leverage SCK for student learning.

Selected Findings

Disciplinary Prowess within Disciplinary Activities

What stood out most to the research team was how both specials candidates seemed to excel when immersed in disciplinary activities—doing athletics or music—with their students. Clinical coaches, regional coordinators, and mentor teachers noticed this as well. After observing Joy, her regional coordinator commented: "[Her] enthusiasm for and love of music transfers easily and naturally to her students." The coordinator went on to note that Joy "cares deeply about what she is teaching."

Kathleen's regional coordinator made a similar comment after watching her teach weight lifting to high school students, stating in her observation feedback that "It is obvious you enjoy the content of the class." Though encouraging, the research team sought evidence for how this disciplinary passion translated into promising instructional practice. Two aspects of the candidates' lessons yielded insights into their developing SCK and its effects on their practice.

Engaging disciplinary richness. First, as one would expect, the primary lesson activities were where the candidates engaged students in the richness and nuance of their respective subjects. During these activities, they could be seen working to unpack concepts and anticipate or adapt to students' various understandings and needs. This required thoughtful consideration about how tools and practices—ingrained into the candidates' repertoires as disciplinary experts—would be taken up by relatively novice teachers.

In designing her elementary music lessons, for example, Joy tried to select songs that were simple enough to illustrate key ideas (e.g., melody and rhythm) but not "kiddish" in a way that would turn students off to participating. To help students learn about these musical concepts, she attempted to draw upon what they already knew and engage them in analogous thinking, such as imagining the ups and downs of melody as being like the Itsy Bitsy Spider moving up and down the waterspout. She then worked to orchestrate group performances, sometimes using instruments, such as drums, glockenspiels, and slide whistles, while maintaining students' focus on the day's musical concept of interest.

Kathleen's jump rope lesson likewise demonstrated her efforts to unpack a commonplace athletic skill for elementary children using recognizable imagery and visualization strategies. As she wrote in her lesson plan:

> We will work on the jump without the rope. Lay your jump rope on the floor and find a sideline. Close your eyes and jump back and forth over the line. What do you hear? Do your feet sound like elephant feet or rabbit feet? For jump roping it is important to be light on your feet.... I will also have students practice swinging their arms with no jump ropes to teach them to keep their arms in. We want to have little chicken wings instead of big bird wings.

Along with clear instructions for what to do with the rope, Kathleen drew upon students' presumed knowledge of animals to give them a sense of the skill objectives. The contrasts she highlighted between elephant and rabbit feet and "little chicken" and "big bird" wings anticipated challenges in student performance and provided accessible language for formatively assessing students during the activity.

Inhabiting familiar roles. Second, the disciplinary nature of instructional activities enabled the candidates to inhabit familiar instructional roles and expert/novice dynamics (Hatano & Oura, 2003). As students played music, for example, Joy sometimes resembled a conductor or a bandleader. Standing before the students, she coordinated their participation in ways that emphasized listening to and building on the contributions of others, much like a band or orchestra operates.

Other times, she came across as a music therapist—a professional role with which she had some experience—by allowing students to create a cathartic cacophony or encouraging them to forge relationships through call-and-response. Compared to these other roles, however, Joy was a teacher charged not only with developing students' conceptual knowledge but also their capacities to learn and reflect upon their learning within a "safe space," as her mentor teacher put it in her feedback on the lesson.

The instructional purchase of inhabiting disciplinary roles was even more pronounced with Kathleen. During her physical education lessons, she sometimes appeared to be assisting individual students much like a coach or overseeing a competition much like a referee. In fact, what the research team felt was her strongest exhibitions of SCK learning emerged during coaching moments. In one poignant example during a lesson on lunge technique within her secondary weight-lifting class, Kathleen carefully observed a student's motions and drew upon her knowledge of a specific sport to offer suggestions for improvement.

She tagged this moment as significant by posting the following comment on Edthena while reviewing the lesson video:

> The student that was asking what their knee should look like during this exercise and since I knew he ran cross country I related it back to something he knows well. This cue allowed him to change his form quickly and have excellent form.

Like a coach, Kathleen provided a quick, targeted cue to initiate a slight but impactful change in an athlete's form to ensure success. But her application of disciplinary knowledge is noteworthy within a classroom context governed by preordained lesson objectives and full of students representing a wide range of sports and athletic experiences and abilities. Indeed, within the same lesson, she also highlighted her cautious efforts to guide another, less athletic student who often resisted feedback. The student, she explained, could "get very frustrated" if she offered too much advice, so she kept it "clear and concise" and allowed him to proceed with poor form because of his "physical limitations."

As a physical education teacher, Kathleen was responsible for building connections for all students given their unique bodies, the lesson objectives, and whatever students might want to get out of the lesson. Unlike a coach, she could not assume a high degree of commitment to a specific sport, an activity, or her discipline more generally. Likewise, Joy could not proceed as if all her students were passionate about music.

Both specials candidates seemed to recognize that interest, passion, and commitment—important aspects of disciplinary knowledge necessary for teaching—had to be designed for and taught to ensure lesson success. The primary activities of the lessons enabled such opportunities for the candidates to model such passion, as they inhabited disciplinary space that was familiar and energizing. In this space, they could be seen leveraging their prowess as a musician or athlete to make the content accessible to students.

Dissonance: Disciplinary Prowess and Doing School

The passion and embodied learning of content that was demonstrated as the specials' candidates engaged students in disciplinary activities contrasted sharply with the moments when they appeared to be *doing school*. Those moments, which included setting up lessons, giving instructions, pacing activities, maintaining student engagement, and administering assessments, were the focus of most of the reflective commentary by both candidates and observers in their feedback.

In reviewing video of her teaching, for example, Joy drew attention to her use of attention-getting cues and admonished herself for things like letting students get "a bit out of control" as they played music. In her Edthena videos, it appeared as though Joy felt compelled to demonstrate classroom management strategies she thought were expected of her. Confirming this expectation, her support team was generally complimentary of her management and highlighted how she focused students on the lesson objectives.

Less frequently, they noted engaged and embodied student learning or highly effective, improvisational teaching (including the moment when Joy perceived things to be "out of control"). As her mentor teacher commented in her lesson feedback, "Joy is very well organized and ready for instruction, and she moves her students briskly through a variety of active, engaging learning activities that involve the 'whole student'—their brains, bodies, and emotions."

Comments and feedback on general schooling practices were no doubt productive for the novices as future teachers. They were also somewhat predictable because the residency program is built, first and foremost, to train teachers (Ball & Forzani, 2009) in the application of essential strategies for delivering effective lessons. This includes research-based, core practices for structuring meaningful learning opportunities for students (McDonald et al., 2013) within the institutional boundaries of contemporary schools.

And, yet, careful review of the data and discussion of SCK learning among the research team revealed a dissonance in the specials candidates' efforts to integrate the more generalized professional practices of teaching and those practices endemic to their particular specials disciplines. Such integration sometimes felt forced and produced questionable outcomes. Two concerns in particular stood out to the research team.

Disconnect between goals and activities. First, the specials candidates seemed to be making content knowledge goals visible for students (and observers) without showing an understanding of how students learn such knowledge. This was evident in Kathleen's forced attempt to include an anticipatory set stressing a conceptual, standards-based objective—heart rates and cardiovascular fitness—more explicitly to her jump rope lesson. Following a generic protocol for planning and implementing lessons, she seemed to think it necessary to always explain the objective to students first before starting the activity, an approach reinforced by observer feedback.

Leveraging the physical dimension of her discipline, it might have been more appropriate to get students moving and, then, at a more appropriate time, draw students' attention to their racing hearts and to insert concepts as needed to facilitate meaningful dialogue and learning. Similarly, after watching herself teach the melody lesson, Joy was worried that she set up her lesson well but did not get to her activity quickly enough or connect performing music with conceptual learning about music in an effective way. It did seem that sometimes she talked too much about concepts, rather than letting participation in musical activity do the teaching and propel the learning, or at least establish meaningful grist for richer, more dialogic discussion with students.

Inauthentic assessments of learning. Second, fitting their lessons to a prescribed formula for good teaching seemed to undermine the specials candidates' sense of how to assess learning within their embodied, creative disciplines. It was especially jarring to see the candidates pivot from engaging students in doing music or physical education activities to having them do more generic forms of written and verbal assessment.

As students playfully used a jump rope in different ways, for example, Kathleen halted the action to remind students to complete a worksheet to track their progress. Students resumed jumping rope, and most of them neglected to fill in the worksheet. In her lesson reflection, Kathleen discussed ways of ensuring student compliance on worksheets in the future. But it is not clear that such compliance would, in fact, increase students' content learning; focusing on strategies for embedded assessment more similar to what a coach might provide novices might have served her better.

Joy also seemed compelled to have students provide evidence of learning that was institutionally legitimate but ill-suited to her discipline. At the end of her lesson on melody, for example, she planned to have students draw a picture of what the concept looked like. Swept up in the singing, she ran out of time and regretted not getting to the "exit ticket." But as her regional coordinator mentioned, it was plainly evident in watching students singing together that they understood how the melody moved "up" and "down."

In another instance, as a way of putting closure on a wonderfully engaging, inquiry-based learning activity on the call-and-response genre and vocal range in the context of singing South African songs, Joy asked students to recite definitions of "call-and-response," "soprano," "alto," "tenor," "base," and several other concepts. As one member of the research team noted after watching the video, the effect of this transition on students was comparable to letting the air out of a balloon. Ironically, a practice meant to ensure learning appeared to impede learning.

Contrasted with the moments when the class was actively engaged in doing music or doing exercise, these teachers' attempts to employ commonplace school-based strategies—presumably to demonstrate they could inhabit the traditional teacher role—were relatively ineffective. More specifically, during these moments, teacher candidates seemed to lose touch with their rich disciplinary knowledge and practice prowess as they apparently attempted to show professional competence.

Concomitantly, students were jolted out of embodied, engaged modes of learning and into decontextualized learning or assessment activities. Witnessing these awkward transitions, it was hard not to wonder what they would have looked like if Joy and Kathleen had been able to remain in the embodied, engaged *frame* and create activity-embedded assessments instead of resorting to more generic, decontextualized assessment strategies.

Importantly, the support team could tell the difference between these modes of engagement, and they liked what they saw when the candidates' teaching was situated more squarely within their disciplines and assessments were embedded within the activities. Despite these insights, however, the support team mostly took a bigger-picture view of the lessons by looking for lesson coherence, specifically how the candidates established clear objectives, taught to them, reminded students of them, and properly assessed them.

Far less common was feedback on how the novice teachers unpacked content *with* students. Again, this was likely at least partially due to the design of the teacher education program, which is tightly tied to multiple sets of learning and teaching standards. Reviewing the findings in light of this design, the researcher team sought to understand this observed dissonance and consider ways that it might be addressed.

Specials Teachers as Special?

In many respects, what was observed of the specials candidates was similar to what has been observed of other teacher candidates: they tend to struggle with the mechanics of teaching a room full of diverse and energetic children. Coordinating or *orchestrating*, as Shulman (1987) termed it, the various components of the job is challenging and takes considerable practice to achieve high levels of success. Presumably, it also takes time to develop specialized content knowledge—to build a repertoire of experiences for understanding how students learn facets of a given discipline. Teacher education can certainly improve its provision of such experiences in the service of ambitious teaching (cf., Lampert et al., 2013).

However, it seems unreasonable to expect candidates to demonstrate complete mastery at interweaving pedagogy and disciplinary knowledge and practice during their residency experience. It is likely to look clunky in the beginning. As such, the dissonance observed may have been evidence of emergence or imperfect progress toward mastery. Eventually, specials candidates might be expected, like any other candidates, to establish instructional routines that maximize students' disciplinary engagement.

Even so, studying specials candidates brought to the forefront how traditional, school-based practices and routines, if rigidly applied, can hamper motivation, engagement, and learning, potentially jeopardizing authentic disciplinary learning opportunities. Just as *good teaching* is not always *just teaching* (Cochran-Smith et al., 2009), viewing teaching through an SCK lens underscores how good teaching should account for disciplinary nuance. As noted earlier, this challenge is not unique to specials.

Reformers across multiple fields have spent decades trying to bring classroom learning experiences into closer alignment with disciplinary norms and practices (see, for example, the aim of having students do science underlying the Next Generation Science Standards [n.d.]). Indeed, all disciplines and the learning experiences they promise risk being undermined by the institutional demands and complexities of doing school (Pierce, 2005; Pope, 2008).

What may be different for many specials teachers, however, is how intimately familiar they are with their disciplines outside of the traditional school environment. Reconciling that familiarity with what they know of schooling and the limitations it presents to their creative, expressive, and embodied fields may prove difficult for some specials candidates.

Most K–12 teachers, especially in the earlier grades, are arguably less likely to have been so immersed within the disciplines they teach as those teaching specials. In their decades of cumulative experience, the research team has rarely encountered teachers with years of experience doing what professional mathematicians, scientists, or writers do. They may have been "good at math" perhaps, but, as a specific form of practice—school math—is at best a simulacrum of the kinds of practice undertaken within the mathematics community (Barab & Duffy, 2000; Lave, 1997).

By comparison, it is not uncommon for physical education teachers to have been athletes or coaches for many years. Likewise, many of the residency program's music and art teachers are accomplished amateurs who are still producing creative works. Forged in disciplinary communities of practice (Wenger, 1998), the identities of such teachers may therefore be more tightly coupled not only with their discipline-specific content knowledge but also with the ways in which that knowledge is learned.

Prospective music teachers, in particular, with their years of focused training, have typically had lengthy apprenticeships that rival or even far outstrip their preparation as beginning teachers (Lortie, 1975). This issue is also common with career changers (in specials fields and other disciplines), who bring with them extensive professional experience.

For teacher educators, then, developing specials candidates' SCK may require more explicit alignment with content-/disciplinary-specific expertise. This raises important questions for the research team in their roles as teacher educators, including: How did the teacher educators in this study learn to be athletes, musicians, or artists? What part did educational preparation programs play in the development of the expertise and disciplinary success? How did school function in similar or different ways from other venues where they developed (and continue to develop) disciplinary expertise?

Teacher candidates in specials subjects may also require a more concerted effort by teacher education programs to establish support networks that scaffold their professional development. Most novice teachers have a difficult time unpacking and assessing content learning, but specials teachers seem to have less curricular and collegial support in schools than their nonspecials colleagues. There are simply fewer potential mentors of specials teachers in most schools and districts. Finding ways to connect those teachers to one another seems crucial, especially for those serving in isolated, rural districts.

Supporting Prospective Specials Teachers

It is easy to forget specials teachers as university-based educators work on multiple fronts to improve teacher preparation. Indeed, it can be useful to step back and consider how candidates and mentor teachers with specialized expertise fit within the ambitious teacher education agenda grounded in core instructional practices derived primarily from studies of math, science, and literacy teaching. The findings reported here underscore the need for supporting specials teachers as they navigate tensions among their fairly sophisticated understanding of content, their emerging understanding of young learners, and their developing pedagogical strategies and skills.

Effective supports would likely make SCK visible to candidates and guide them to thoughtfully integrate SCK into their designs for learning. This might entail building upon familiar disciplinary roles and modes of instruction, such as having prospective music teachers consider the relationship between classroom teaching and being an orchestra conductor (Forrester, 2018). Teacher educators might also draw attention to assumptions about how disciplinary knowledge is learned and how this knowledge influences one's teaching (for an example, in music teacher preparation, see Raiber & Teachout, 2014; for physical education teacher preparation, see Ward et al., 2014).

Likewise, tools, such as content maps, can be co-developed by teacher educators, mentor teachers, and content experts to guide and assess candidates' ability to leverage SCK to meet students' diverse learning needs (Ward et al., 2015). To enable such leveraging, teacher educators should push candidates to strengthen their repertoire of authentic disciplinary practices, to trouble or deconstruct generic teaching strategies, and to imagine and enact more embodied, dynamic modes of teaching, learning, and assessment. As this chapter demonstrates, collaborative inquiry by a teacher education team can unearth those generic strategies and ensure the unique qualities of music, physical education, and other specials subjects remain central to the learning experience for licensure candidates and their students.

References

Ball, D. L., & Forzani, F. M. (2009). The work of teaching and the challenge for teacher education. *Journal of Teacher Education*, 60(5), 497–511.

Ball, D. L., Thames, M. H., & Phelps, G. (2008). Content knowledge for teaching: What makes it special? *Journal of Teacher Education*, 59(5), 389–407.

Barab, S. A., & Duffy, T. M. (2000). From practice fields to communities of practice. In D. H. Jonassen & S. M. Land (Eds.), *Theoretical foundations of learning environments* (pp. 25–55). Mahwah, NJ: Lawrence Erlbaum Associates.

Berry, A., Friedrichsen, P., & Loughran, J. (2015). *Re-examining pedagogical content knowledge in science education*. New York: Routledge.

Cochran-Smith, M., & Lytle, S. L. (2009). *Inquiry as stance: Practitioner research for the next generation*. New York: Teachers College Press.

Cochran-Smith, M., Shakman, K., Jong, C., Terrell, D. G., Barnatt, J., & McQuillan, P. (2009). Good and just teaching: The case for social justice in teacher education. *American Journal of Education*, 115(3), 347–377.

Forrester, S. H. (2018). Music teacher knowledge: An examination of the intersections between instrumental music teaching and conducting. *Journal of Research in Music Education*, 65(4), 461–482.

Graham, G., Parker, S., Wilkins, J. L., Fraser, R., Westfall, S., & Tembo, M. (2002). The effects of high-stakes testing on elementary school art, music, and physical education. *Journal of Physical Education, Recreation and Dance*, 73(8), 51–54.

Grossman, P., Wineburg, S., & Woolworth, S. (2001). Toward a theory of teacher community. *Teachers College Record*, 103(6), 942–1012. http://doi.org/10.1111/0161-4681.00140

Hatano, G., & Oura, Y. (2003). Commentary: Reconceptualizing school learning using insight from expertise research. *Educational Researcher*, 32(8), 26–29.

Lampert, M., Franke, M. L., Kazemi, E., Ghousseini, H., Turrou, A. C., Beasley, H., Cunard, A., & Crowe, K. (2013). Keeping it complex: Using rehearsals to support novice teacher learning of ambitious teaching. *Journal of Teacher Education, 64*(3), 226–243.

Lave, J. (1997). The culture of acquisition and the practice of understanding. In D. Kirshner and J. A. Whitson (Eds.), *Situated cognition: Social, semiotic, and psychological perspectives* (pp. 17–36). Mahwah, NJ: Lawrence Erlbaum.

Lortie, D. C. (1975). *Schoolteacher: A sociological study.* Chicago, IL: University of Chicago Press.

McDonald, M., Kazemi, E., & Kavanagh, S. S. (2013). Core practices and pedagogies of teacher education: A call for a common language and collective activity. *Journal of Teacher Education, 64*(5), 378–386.

McNeil, L. (2000). *Contradictions of school reform: Educational costs of standardized testing.* New York: Routledge.

Next Generation Science Standards. (n.d.). *Understanding the standards.* https://www.nextgenscience.org/understanding-standards/understanding-standards

Pierce, K. M. (2005). Posing, pretending, waiting for the bell: Life in high school classrooms. *The High School Journal, 89*(2), 1–15.

Pope, D. C. (2008). *Doing school: How we are creating a generation of stressed out, materialistic, and miseducated students.* New Haven, CT: Yale University Press.

Raiber, M., & Teachout, D. (2014). *The journey from music student to teacher: A professional approach.* New York: Routledge.

Shulman, L. S. (1987). Knowledge and teaching: Foundations of the new reform. *Harvard Educational Review, 57,* 1–22.

Stake, R. E. (1995). *The art of case study research.* Thousand Oaks, CA: Sage.

Stake, R. E. (2005). Qualitative case studies. In N. K. Denzin & Y. S. Lincoln (Eds.), *The Sage handbook of qualitative research* (pp. 443–466). Thousand Oaks, CA: Sage.

Ward, P., Ayvazo, S., & Lehwald, H. (2014). Using knowledge packets in teacher education to develop pedagogical content knowledge. *Journal of Physical Education, Recreation and Dance, 85*(6), 38–43.

Ward, P., Lehwald, H., & Lee, Y. S. (2015). Content maps: A teaching and assessment tool for content knowledge. *Journal of Physical Education, Recreation and Dance, 86*(5), 38–46.

Wenger, E. (1998). *Communities of practice: Learning, meaning, and identity.* Cambridge, UK: Cambridge University Press.

West, C. (2012). Teaching music in an era of high-stakes testing and budget reductions. *Arts Education Policy Review, 113*(2), 75–79.

CHAPTER TWO

Improving Educator Preparation Using Asynchronous, Online Professional Development

Allison R. Magagnosc and Ingrid T. Everett

This chapter describes how a three-year, state-funded, eligible partnership grant awarded to an institute of higher education (IHE) in central Pennsylvania worked to align state priorities and regulations with the knowledge and pedagogy of teacher candidates and their clinical internship support team, specifically, mentor teachers, principals, and university-based teacher educators.

The project, referred to as Pre-Service Differently (PSD), provided over 50 hours of professional development (PD) to the clinical internship support team so they could model best teaching practices and provide evidence-based resources to teacher candidates during their culminating sixteen-week, school-based, clinical internship. The PD consisted of online, asynchronous modules completed independently, at any time and in any order, in addition to virtual coaching, which enabled teachers to participate independent of geographic location. As a result of their participation, teachers reported implementing evidence-based practices more frequently, and their confidence in supporting teacher candidates increased.

Clinical Internship Support Team

PSD offered the asynchronous PD to teacher candidates' clinical internship support team, which included teachers, principals, and university-based teacher educators. Project developers drew similar conclusions to Portelance et al.'s (2016) case study, in which mentor teachers and university-based teacher educators had the greatest impact on their teacher candidate when they engaged in collaborative dialogue that elaborated on each other's prior comments and included examples from their unique perspectives.

Similarly, Slick (1998) found that, when university-based teacher educators and mentor teachers worked together in crafting opportunities for teacher candidates, the university-based teacher educator was less likely to feel like an "outsider" simply there to serve as a "sounding board" (p. 831), providing the teacher candidate with more effective support.

Knowing that teacher candidates' content knowledge, specifically in math, science, and English/Language Arts, can impact student achievement (Hill et al., 2005), PSD also sought to provide an additional university-based, content-specific educator to co-supervise teacher candidates placed in secondary schools for their clinical internship. Despite interest from content-area faculty, the logistics of coordinating time for two individuals to observe teacher candidates were unrealistic.

In total, 158 teachers, 25 principals, and 2 university-based teacher educators engaged in the PD. By the end of the three-year grant, 123 teachers, 12 principals, and 1 university-based teacher educator had completed all of the PD requirements. The majority of teachers (78%) and 48% of principals who started, completed the PD. Teachers with or expecting a teacher candidate had higher PD completion rates than teachers without a teacher candidate in part because they wanted to learn and have the most up-to-date resources when working with a teacher candidate (Rudolph & Feighan, 2016).

Participants hailed from 24 school districts in central Pennsylvania, nine of which had a low-income student population over 50%. The majority of participants (64%) had been teaching for over 12 years, and 20% had been teaching between 8 and 11 years. They taught at every grade level (kindergarten through 12th grade); one-quarter of the participants taught special education. Across five semesters, the IHE placed 171 teacher candidates in a clinical internship with a teacher who participated in PSD. Participation may have been higher had the following considerations for recruitment been understood sooner.

Recruitment Considerations

To ensure the clinical internship support team receives training prior to the teacher candidates' clinical internship, sufficient time must be provided for the recruitment and engagement of participants in PD. The intention was for mentor teachers to complete the PD modules before their assigned teacher candidate began their clinical experience. However, the PD typically took one year to complete. Therefore, teacher candidates paired with a PSD mentor teacher, especially in the first year, did not receive the benefit of a mentor who completed the PD.

Another challenge arose if teacher candidates' placement needs did not match the certification area of teachers who had completed the PD, which created the possibility that a teacher candidate was not paired with a trained teacher. If PSD had not used the first year as a pilot, recruiting only a few participants, and instead had engaged a larger number of people to begin the PD earlier, more teacher candidates could have had a trained mentor teacher.

Beyond recruitment of participants, some school districts had rigid policies about placing teacher candidates, which prevented consecutive placements with a PSD-trained mentor teacher. Such challenges highlight the importance of considering school districts' teacher candidate placement policies when choosing partners and designing an intervention. Ultimately, PSD might have had a greater impact than what emerged from the data had recruitment considerations been understood.

Data and Methods

The findings referenced in this chapter include data collected as part of the grant-funded program evaluation completed by an external evaluator. Participants completed surveys before and after engaging in the PD; questions included self-reported teaching practices and feedback about the PD. In addition, the evaluator conducted focus groups with participants, PD developers, coaching staff, and the grant's project manager to better understand the experiences of participants and areas for improvement.

Professional Development

PSD collaborated with one of the state's Intermediate Units (IU) to develop and disseminate the PD. The IUs are legislatively created, regional educational service agencies that serve schools and districts and liaise with the state's Department of Education (DOE). IUs are uniquely situated to address the instructional and operational needs of their communities. Staff in the Curriculum Services and Professional Development Department supported PSD by curating the PD and providing the instructional coaching for participants.

Professional Development Format

Participants engaged in the PD online through staff developed presentations and a curated selection of virtual learning experiences, herein referred to as modules. PSD used the open source learning platform Moodle as the hub where participants viewed module descriptions, found links to access each module, and tracked their progress. Moodle also allowed participants to virtually interact with project staff and other participants through public message boards.

The learning modules consisted of a variety of virtual activities that addressed each module's learning goal. In some cases, activities included accessing freely available webinars from EduPlanet21 and the Center for Schools and Communities. For other topics, participants accessed literature or videos and then wrote reflections about how the content translated to their teaching practice.

Teachers appreciated the flexibility afforded by asynchronous, online learning (Erickson, et al., 2012; Parsons et al., 2019; Rudolph & Feighan, 2016). Since each module was distinct in content, it was not necessary to dictate the order in which participants completed it. This allowed participants to choose topics most salient to their needs. Participants could also start and progress through the activities when the time best suited them. For many teachers, the summer break provided the time needed to complete all the modules.

As reported on the feedback survey administered after completing the PD, the majority of 160 survey respondents agreed that the PD activities were of sufficient intensity (94%) and met their needs (96%) (Rudolph & Feighan, 2016). Specifically, there was a wide variety of activities and resources that made participants think and reflect on their practice and stay engaged in the PD. Participants also valued the availability of external resources for when they wanted to learn more about a topic. With all of the resources online, it was easy for participants to log in and reference materials as they became pertinent to their teaching or their teacher candidates' growth.

On the surveys after the PD was completed, one mentor teacher described how she felt "more confident in all of these areas that the module addressed and can sufficiently answer any questions my student teacher has or will have." The PD provided mentor teachers with the most up-to-date, research-based practices that they could model and share with their teacher candidates.

Professional Development Format Considerations

The order in which PSD presented the learning opportunities had an impact on participant retention. The module listed first on promotional materials and on Moodle was one of the most time-consuming, and the content was dry. As a result, only about half (56%) of the 333 people who received login credentials and completed the presurvey, went on to complete at least one module. Although participants were informed that they could complete the modules in the order of their choosing, the vast majority of participants completed them in the order presented.

Jones (2013) recommended that the first PD module should be engaging and allow for a high degree of success. To that end, a PSD staff member shared with those recently enrolled suggestions for module sequence found to be successful by prior participants. The platform for accessing the PD must be easy for participants to navigate since it greatly influences educators' participation and their perceptions of the learning experience (Macià & García, 2016).

While Moodle served as a consistent starting point, participants had to log in to an additional external website with separate credentials to access much of the PD content. Upon completion of the experience on the external websites, participants had to navigate back to Moodle and indicate completion. This manual process often left participants confused about their progress because many forgot to update Moodle. A drawback to the PD as designed was the requirement for participants to track their own progress. Any system that is deployed should consistently and automatically update participant progress.

Participants had autonomy to complete the PD as their schedule allowed, but the online nature reduced external accountability. Similarly, without regularly scheduled dates and times for engaging in PD, participants often lost momentum or did not complete the PD. To support participants in completing the PD as intended, project developers should provide or have participants establish a timeline for completion that includes shorter-term goals.

Participants had multiple motivations for completing the PD, and a monetary incentive was the primary driver of module completion. Participants also received continuing education credits, and PSD celebrated participants by posting photographs of those who received their certificate of completion. In addition, Jones (2013) found that perceived or actual organizational support for PD can lead to increased completion rates and higher satisfaction with the learning experience. To that end, PSD obtained permission to solicit staff involvement from district superintendents and then visited schools to explain the opportunity in detail.

Professional Development Content
Topics were chosen to align with the parameters of the grant, which included addressing findings from a needs assessment conducted in local school

districts, and statewide priorities, such as the Danielson Framework and the Common Core Standards. In addition, much of the PD focused on supporting educators in understanding and more successfully using the DOE's Standards Aligned System (SAS), which consisted of six factors identified as having a positive effect on student achievement: standards, assessment, curriculum framework, instruction, materials and resources, and safe and supportive schools (Tanney, 2010).

One module provided an overview of the SAS website and how each factor supported continuous improvement and student achievement. Participants gained exposure to each factor and the publicly available resources they could use to improve their instruction. Subsequent modules provided more in-depth information about each of the six SAS factors. For example, participants learned about effective and engaging standards-based instruction in addition to methods to help ensure that all students met the state's Common Core standards and learned to value critical thinking.

In another module, participants were introduced to the *Framework for Teaching*, created by Charlotte Danielson (2011), and learned about how the rubric could serve as the foundation for deeper understanding of their roles and responsibilities as an educator. Next, they learned about the observation process, reflected on being assessed using the framework, and selected two activities that served to further enhance their knowledge and understanding about a component of the framework. Participants appreciated learning strategies they could implement to reach the next level on the rubric, such as shifting ownership of the learning to students.

One module sought to support participants' development and use of assessments to improve instruction. Participants reflected on whether their current practices promoted student achievement, and then they learned some introductory strategies for creating formative and summative assessments. In a following module, participants gained tools for making instructional decisions based on data and learned about how data can inform school-level decisions. On the post survey, participants expressed the value of learning about a variety of data sources, especially those beyond standardized test data.

Another module focused on the formulation of safe, bully-free environments. Participants watched a series of webinars that provided examples of bullying that occurred in schools and articulated the importance of creating a safe learning environment. Participants learned about proactive approaches to bullying prevention, including collaboration with their community and students' families. The content also included legal explanations and ramifications. Participants described an increase in their awareness of and attention to bullying actions and appreciated the ability to brainstorm with other teachers about strategies to address bullying.

Finally, in alignment with the Council for the Accreditation of Educator Preparation (CAEP, 2018) Standard 3, participants learned about digital resources that they could use to promote learning in and out of the classroom. Resources included how to build a website and blog, educational iPad applications, and strategies for flipped classrooms, among other examples. Teachers' perceived impact of this module varied. While some teachers described how they planned to embed the resources they learned into their lessons, others did not feel as though they were appropriate for the age level they taught or their school did not have the technology to support the resources they learned about.

Professional Development Results

A comparison of participant pre- and post-survey responses revealed an increase in self-reported frequency of implementation/engagement in a variety of teaching practices. For example, 86% of the 94 respondents used appropriate and current technology for instructional purposes, compared to 64% before. They also were more likely to use the Common Core standards to plan lessons and use formative, summative, and diagnostic assessment strategies to understand students' learning.

After engaging in the PD, 78% of people agreed that their students actively participated in classroom activities and achieved higher levels than students in previous years, an increase from 60% of respondents before. One teacher, in a focus group, explained how she began holding students to a higher standard of work and reported that students met the higher standards. Similarly, after the PD, 9 in 10 respondents agreed that they could maintain a safe classroom environment, free from bullying.

Participants also reflected on their increased ability to work with teacher candidates. Before the PD, only half of respondents reported frequently using appropriate coaching strategies, but after the PD 78% reported doing so. After the PD, 71% of participants frequently assisted current or future teachers in collecting, analyzing, and using student data to improve their teaching practices, compared to only 56% before. One mentor teacher explained how the PD "has made me more mindful of the necessary teacher qualifications . . . so that I can better encourage those traits" in the teacher candidates.

Another mentor teacher described how her teacher candidate was unfamiliar with the Danielson framework. However, after she had completed the module, she was able to provide the teacher candidate with detailed information about the framework. Overall, mentor teachers described feeling more confident in supporting a teacher candidate armed with the information provided in the PD.

Professional Development Content Considerations

As recruitment of participants expanded to new geographic areas, the staff's PD needs differed. PSD in collaboration with the local IU identified appropriate existing modules or developed offerings to disseminate through the PSD system. Many of the topics expanded on the original content with a focus on meeting the needs of a more diverse student population.

For example, in addition to the original offerings about standards-based instruction, participants could engage in modules about culturally responsive instruction, understanding students through their cultural lens, and creating a community of learners. Other modules provided additional training on data-informed decision-making, including four types of data (student/family demographics, perceptions, student learning, and school/district processes) that can provide insights into a school's performance.

As additional content became available, participants had the freedom to choose any topics that were relevant to their professional growth. Once the modules were created, they became available for continued use. For example, as teacher candidates transitioned to teachers of record, they had a resource available to supplement their induction support.

PSD Instructional Coaching Experience

With grant funding, project personnel completed a Letter of Endorsement in Teacher Leadership and Instructional Coaching—a joint collaboration between the National Institute for Professional Practice and a local university. The endorsement covered many strategies for meeting the needs of adult learners, such as how to facilitate change using reflective practice and understanding the mentee's school culture (Knight, 2015).

The culminating course used case study examples from multiple grade levels, content areas, and special needs populations to challenge coaches to apply their instructional coaching skills in a variety of situations. One newly trained coach reflected in a focus group conversation that "my repertoire of instructional strategies and links and resources has just grown tremendously." The training of instructional coaches provided the expertise and necessary skills to effectively coach participating teachers, principals, and university-based teacher educators.

PSD engaged participants in a minimum of 10 hours of one-on-one coaching after completion of the online modules. A review of 35 studies of effective PD confirmed the critical nature of instructional coaching (Darling-

Hammond et al., 2017) because it can impact school culture, facilitate lasting change through reflection and decision-making, and acknowledge the competence of adult learners (Toll, 2005).

With this in mind, PSD-trained coaches knowledgeable in both the pedagogy and content taught during the PD facilitated a respectful connection (Darling-Hammond et al., 2017; Tooley & Connally, 2016) and developed a foundational, trusting relationship with participants (Knight, 2015). PSD also aimed to balance educator self-direction with the input of experts (Spelman et al., 2016; Tooley and Connally, 2016) by having participants provide their coach with challenges or topics they would like to explore in more detail and collaboratively deciding on the focus for coaching.

Initially, the coaching was to take place, at least in part, face-to-face. After the first year, participants completed the PD in increasingly larger numbers, placing an undue burden on the coaches. As a result, all instructional coaching occurred virtually through email, phone, and conferencing software. In a focus group, one participant stated, "[it] was nice being able to communicate via email. It didn't always need to be in person. . . . it was really convenient and easy to use."

One coach described how for many participants this was the first time they had used conferencing software. Following initial trepidation, participants felt comfortable and successfully used the technology. That experience also served as an example of how teachers can access resources beyond their school building, which was one learning goal from the module about technology.

Since coaches did not need to travel, they could spend more time compiling resources and crafting learning experiences. The coach provided resources, including videos, webinars, and websites along with reflection and action items, to support each teacher's continued learning and change in practice. For example, participants worked with their coach on improving their instruction for all students, including gifted or high-achieving students. Others looked for support in creating cross-curricular connections and improving reading comprehension in social studies and science. Teachers also focused on including project-based learning, hybrid learning, and reteaching into their pedagogical practice.

Results of the Coaching

Participating teachers appreciated the individualized support their coaches provided. In a focus group, one coach summarized teachers' reactions as "really excited about having someone really focus the attention on them and their needs in order to address the needs of their students." Teachers also valued discussing the challenges they were facing, gaining new resources or perspectives, and trying out new approaches in a low-stakes environment.

Coaches also directly or indirectly supported teacher candidates. One mentor teacher in a focus group described how she worked with her coach to obtain ideas to support her teacher candidate. The mentor teacher and teacher candidate would reflect on the resources together, and then the mentor teacher would discuss the experience with her coach. In another case, the coach provided a mentor teacher with resources on the gradual release model in coaching as well as the theory of conscious and competence learning model. These resources served as tools the mentor teacher used when working with her teacher candidate.

Instructional Coaching Considerations
Since instructional coaches are important links between theory and implementation (Spelman et al., 2016), identifying qualified educators in participating school districts who are willing to complete the instructional coaching qualification and serve as a resource for mentor teachers is strongly recommended. If mentor teachers are supported by a coach who is "physically present and engaged in supporting, encouraging and guiding them" (Spelman et al., 2016, p. 32), change in their practice is more likely.

Conclusion

PSD supported teacher candidates' clinical internship support team by providing online, asynchronous PD and virtual instructional coaching. The format enabled educators to participate irrespective of their geographic location. Participants also appreciated the ability to choose the PD modules and topics for coaching that would most benefit them, their teacher candidate, and ultimately their students. Virtual coaching sessions provided PSD with a viable way to provide individualized support to a large number of participants so that they could translate what they learned in the PD into practice.

While participants had the flexibility to choose the time and order in which they completed the PD, the format of the online system posed challenges for retention. Also, the timing for recruitment, participation in PD, and teacher candidates' field placement must be carefully considered. Providing up-to-date resources and best practices to the clinical internship support team allowed them to work together using the same language when working with a teacher candidate.

Mentor teachers also gained confidence and mentoring tools for when they worked with their teacher candidate. In addition, they self-reported an increase in the frequency for which they employed teaching practices learned during the PD. Once the online system is in place, new modules can be added as participants needs and state priorities evolve. In addition, once the content is created, it can easily be shared with new mentor teachers and teacher candidates as they become teachers of record, allowing the IHEs to sustain support for teacher candidates and novice teacher induction.

References

Council for the Accreditation of Educator Preparation. (2018, May). *CAEP handbook: Initial-level programs 2018.* http://caepnet.org/~/media/Files/caep/accreditation-resources/caep-initial-handbook-2018.pdf?la=en

Danielson, C. (2011). *The framework for teaching: Evaluation instrument.* Princeton, NJ: Danielson Group.

Darling-Hammond, L., Hyler, M. E., & Gardner, M. (2017, June 5). *Effective teacher professional development.* Learning Policy Institute. https://learningpolicyinstitute.org/sites/default/files/product-files/Effective_Teacher_Professional_Development_REPORT.pdf

Erickson, A., Noonan, P., & McCall, Z. (2012). Effectiveness of online professional development for rural special educators. *Rural Special Education Quarterly, 31*(1), 22–32.

Hill, H. C., Rowan, B., & Ball, D. L. (2005). Effects of teachers' mathematical knowledge for teaching on student achievement. *American Educational Research Journal, 42*(2), 371–406.

Jones, A. (2013). Increasing adult learner motivation for completing self-directed e-learning. *Performance Improvement, 52*(7), 32–42.

Knight, J. (2015). Teach to win: Seven success factors for instructional coaching programs. *Principal Leadership, 15*(7), 24–27.

Macià, M., & García, I. (2016). Informal online communities and networks as a source of teacher professional development: A review. *Teaching and Teacher Education, 55,* 291–307.

Parsons, S., Hutchison, A., Hall, L., Parsons, A., Ives, S., & Leggett, A. (2019). U.S. teachers' perceptions of online professional development. *Teaching and Teacher Education, 82,* 33–42.

Portelance, L., Caron, J., & Martineau, S. (2016). Collaboration through knowledge sharing between cooperating teachers and university supervisors. *Brock Education Journal, 26*(1).

Rudolph, A., & Feighan, K. (2016). *Pre-service differently final evaluation report, 2013–2016.* Public Health Management Corporation (PHMC).

Slick, S. (1998). The university supervisor: A disenfranchised outsider. *Teaching and Teacher Education, 14*(8), 821–834.

Spelman, M., Bell, D., Thomas, E., & Briody, J. (2016). Combining professional development & instructional coaching to transform the classroom environment in PreK–3 classrooms. *Journal of Research in Innovative Teaching*, 9(1), 30–46.

Tanney, A. (2010). Singing out of the same songbook: The standards aligned system in Pennsylvania. Lincoln, IL: Center on Innovation & Improvement.

Toll, C. (2005). *The literacy coach's survival guide: Essential questions and practical answers*. Newark, DE: International Reading Association.

Tooley, M., & Connally, K. (2016). *No panacea: Diagnosing what ails teacher professional development before reaching for remedies*. https://files.eric.ed.gov/fulltext/ED570895.pdf

CHAPTER THREE

A Model of Collaboration

Mentor Teachers, Teacher Candidates, and University-Based Teacher Educators

Deborah Yost, Greer M. Richardson, Thomas R. Conway, Allison R. Magagnosc, and Alana M. Mellor

Research demonstrates an urgent need for teacher education programs to work closely with mentor teachers to provide expert mentoring during the clinical internship to build resiliency among teacher candidates and reduce teacher attrition (He, 2009; Richardson et al., 2019). The American Association of Colleges for Teacher Education (AACTE, 2018) calls for a "Rigorous selection of clinical educators and coaches from both higher education and the PK–12 sector" (p. 5).

Still, others propose that teacher preparation programs take on the added responsibility to develop inservice teachers as expert mentors since the clinical internship is one of the most important experiences shaping teacher candidate beliefs and confidence (Hammerness et al., 2005; Richardson et al., 2019; Sayeski & Paulsen, 2012; Smith & Avetisian, 2011).

Although there is a dearth of research on the effect of expert mentoring on teacher candidate development, research does exist that attests to the efficacy of mentor development (Richardson et al., 2019). Research has also shown that relationships among mentor teachers, teacher candidates, and others in the school environment increase the overall efficacy and satisfaction of the clinical internship experience (Greiman, 2007; Russell & Russell, 2011; Sayeski & Paulsen, 2012; Wanberg et al., 2003).

While there is a great deal of research on expert mentoring, the literature primarily focuses on mentoring new teachers (Dyson, 2010; He, 2009; Wang & Odell, 2002). However, recent attention has focused on providing mentor teachers with knowledge of expert mentoring for teacher candidates using an instructional coaching model (Richardson et al., 2019). Expert mentoring centers on equal partnerships between mentor teachers and teacher candidates to stimulate mutual reflection on teaching practice. Similarly, the instructional coaching relationship is collaborative, democratic, reflective, and mutually beneficial (Aguilar, 2013; Knight, 2007).

This chapter provides an overview of a multifaceted set of strategies primarily aimed at inculcating expert mentoring/coaching strategies among mentor teachers during a three-year (2013–2016) Pennsylvania Department of Education grant-funded, multi-institutional partnership known as the Greater Philadelphia Instructional Coaching Program (GPIC).

The grant sought to create a climate of distributed leadership in participating schools through the development of professional learning communities (PLCs) led by mentor teachers schooled in instructional coaching (IC) strategies. The program goals included:

- Creating strong partnerships between institutes of higher education (IHEs) and local schools and between principals, mentor teachers, and university-based teacher educators.
- Developing and implementing coursework that provided evidence-based IC practices and firsthand experience mentoring teacher candidates and peers.
- Supporting school communities by scaffolding the use of PLCs and inviting multidisciplinary faculty to provide professional development (PD).

The chapter begins with an overview of the partnership grant, followed by a discussion of the work each institution did to support teacher candidates and their mentor teachers. Because mentor teachers, principals, and university-based teacher educators enrolled in IC coursework together, a detailed explanation of each course in the IC sequence is outlined. Next, an overview of the grant's PLC work is presented, followed by a discussion of results and findings. Finally, results on the model's signature instructional coaching practices conclude the chapter to provide key elements of a successful model of mentor teacher development.

A Positive Multi-Institutional Partnership

The grant evolved from early work on teacher leadership/instructional coaching conducted by professors at the lead institution (Yost et al., 2010). In the study, existing middle school literacy/mathematics coordinators were trained to use instructional coaching strategies in their work with practicing teachers, which resulted in an increase in teaching efficacy among teachers, benchmark scores, and standardized test scores. Based on this work, the primary author designed a four-course, graduate, instructional coach endorsement certification program, which led to using the endorsement to educate mentor teachers to coach teacher candidates during the clinical internship experience.

The GPIC program was a partnership of four IHEs that agreed to work together to improve educational outcomes for teacher candidates. Each IHE made contractual agreements among itself and with K–8 school sites, clarifying the expectations of the partnerships that would be forged. Twelve university-based teacher educators were recruited to work alongside mentor teachers and teacher candidates to form strong tripartite relationships. Across the four IHEs, the project recruited six arts and science and education faculty to support 48 site-specific, needs-based PD sessions at area schools.

In all, GPIC contracted with 20 schools that served 3,500 students. Partner schools agreed to (1) serve as clinical placements for teacher candidates; (2) identify up to six potential teacher leaders to learn expert mentoring skills through the IC endorsement, who would also provide turnaround training for mentor teachers in their buildings; and (3) support PLCs developed by mentor teachers as practicing instructional coaches. As a result, 22 building leaders and 120 mentor teachers supported 140 teacher candidates during their clinical internship.

In an effort to track the partners' overall satisfaction of the partnership, the Partnership Self-Assessment Tool (National Collaborating Centre for Methods and Tools, 2008) was administered in the second and third years of the grant. Overall, participants, who included principals, university-based teacher educators, faculty, and the grant management team, expressed satisfaction with the program and the partnership's ability to implement the program and achieve its goals.

All of the partners agreed that they developed new skills and valuable relationships and were able to utilize their expertise to have a greater impact than they could have had on their own. Respondents rated the project leadership favorably, and while synergy was the lowest-rated area, it still received a relatively positive score. When participant groups were viewed separately, principals held the least positive perceptions of the program, while IHE faculty held the highest perceptions of the program.

A Common Language for Teacher Candidate Assessment

Because the clinical internship is both instructive and evaluative, one of GPIC's priorities included aligning teacher candidate assessments with the state's teacher evaluation system and providing PD to ensure that the teacher mentors trained as instructional coaches, teacher candidates, and university-based educators had common knowledge and shared language entering into the clinical internship. To that end, each of the IHE's educator preparation programs adopted the Danielson framework (Danielson, 2011) as the primary instrument to provide feedback to teacher candidates during the clinical semester.

Each team, which included the teacher candidate, university-based teacher educator, and mentor teacher, attended a daylong PD to learn about the Danielson framework, with follow-up workshops in coursework and during teacher candidate seminars, to enhance confidence in their use of the rubric and guide coaching discussions with teacher candidates. It was important that teacher candidates learn how they would be evaluated during their internship experience to ensure a smooth transition into teaching.

Through supplemental seminars, teacher candidates also developed knowledge about other teacher evaluation strategies, such as building-level data, teacher-specific data on student learning over a three-year span from Pennsylvania's Value-Added Assessment System (PVAAS), and progress on Student Learning Objectives (SLO) prior to their first year of teaching. During these seminars, teacher candidates also reviewed Response to Intervention (RTI) systems, Common Core Standards, and data-based decision-making related to student learning and achievement.

All content was aligned to the mentor teachers' IC endorsement coursework and was intended to advance the knowledge of teacher candidates for the realities of the school in which they would teach. Embedding assessment content into both teacher candidate seminars and IC coursework was a crucial factor in teacher candidates' knowledge of how teachers are evaluated. As well, mentor teachers were required to gain a deeper understanding of the Danielson framework and to use it as a discussion tool in their conferences with teacher candidates, thus increasing their understanding of how to improve their own teaching practices using this tool. The following sections provide an overview of the development and aligned content in IC coursework.

In the first year of the program, the lead institution ran the IC coursework and content-area PD for the first cohort of mentor teachers, while the other IHE partners developed their own programs and applied for their own IC endorsement. Subsequently, all four teacher educator programs replicated the offerings for the second cohort of mentor teachers. The program's tiered approach allowed the project to be developed jointly and replicated broadly in a short period of time.

An Instructional Coaching Endorsement Framework

All four IC courses were created in hybrid format, with four-hour live sessions every other week interspersed with virtual sessions over a 10-week period. In the first cohort, one faculty member from each IHE collaboratively planned and taught these courses. Mentor teachers, principals, and university-based teacher educators completed the first two introductory courses together to establish enhanced relationships among these professionals; develop a common language around coaching; and, ultimately, better support teacher candidates.

Only mentor teachers went on to complete the final two courses since the content of these courses focused solely on their role as instructional coaches to teacher candidates and informal teacher leaders within their schools. Each course in the IC endorsement required mentor teachers to add content completed in coursework to a portfolio aligned with the Pennsylvania standards for IC endorsement. Portfolio guidelines are depicted in table 3.1.

Table 3.1. Portfolio Guidelines

IC Endorsement Standard	Included Items
Content	Pennsylvania Framework for Standards; specific knowledge of standards-based instruction; research-based instruction; Common Core Standards; adult learning and professional development practices.
Instructional Coaching Skills and Abilities	Coaching approaches, barriers to effective coaching, conferring cycles with teachers, analyze instructional/behavioral practices, plan collaboratively with teachers, model classroom practices, demonstrate understanding of adult learners, and reflect on own work.
Instructional Practices	Co-teaching, effective coaching on integration of technology, becoming reflective practitioners, instructional planning, appropriate selection and implementation of instructional tools/strategies, formal and informal assessment, culturally responsive pedagogy/management, and classroom management.

(continued)

Table 3.1. *(continued)*

IC Endorsement Standard	Included Items
Assessment	Use assessment from multiple measures to guide instruction, monitor results of interventions, and alter instruction accordingly; effectively use technology in assessment and data analysis; use multiple assessment strategies to measure student mastery; and design assessments that target standards in subject areas.
Organizational Leadership and School Change	Understand school change literature regarding schools as communities of learners, exhibit interpersonal skills to promote student learning, listen effectively to inspire trust, work collaboratively with school leadership to promote common goals and school vision, work collaboratively with colleagues in setting goals for school improvement/reform and promoting shared leadership in the school, and communicate with internal and external audiences (e.g., parents and community members)

The portfolio served as a culminating assessment tool for the program and a reminder of the key areas of content covered in the IC endorsement. The following section outlines each three-credit graduate-level course in the IC program.

Course One: Introduction to Instructional Leadership

The research shows very clearly that developing teachers as instructional coaches requires a solid understanding of leadership, differential coaching models, and how to analyze data (Aguilar, 2013; Knight, 2007; Yost et al., 2010). The first course promoted a deep understanding of the roles and responsibilities of an IC. All participants explored the fundamentals of (1) educational leadership and distributed leadership, (2) coaching models and how to differentiate coaching, (3) working with adult learners and supporting reflective practice, (4) data-based decision-making and RTI models, and (5) models of consultation and professional development.

All assignments connected learning to the school environment. For example, mentor teachers were asked to reflect on their schools' RTI model and its effectiveness in increasing student learning and achievement as well as discussing how their role of IC might increase the effectiveness of the model. Moreover, they reflected on personal experiences with PD in light of the latest research and created a school-based PD improvement plan. Participants wrote a journal on effective coaching strategies and completed a data analysis project based on school or classroom data.

Course Two: Advanced Instructional Design

As the research shows, all potential coaches should revisit "good" teaching and management practices prior to coaching a teacher candidate (Marzano & Simms, 2013; Yost et al., 2010). The second course inculcated a deep understanding of evidence-based instructional and management practices, specifically, how students learn, aspects of lesson planning, information processing, motivation/self-efficacy, Common Core Standards, and culturally proficient teaching and management practices. Assignments focused on translating best practices learned first among peers.

For example, participants worked in small groups to plan a lesson using an evidence-based strategy and then taught and videotaped the lesson. The whole group completed an analysis of the lesson based on Danielson's framework. Similarly, mentor teachers wrote an ongoing blog on their future roles as ICs related to the primary Danielson domains: Planning and Instruction, Classroom, Environment, and Instruction. For another assignment, teachers worked collaboratively to create chapters of a class book on successful lessons related to Common Core, which was distributed digitally to the entire class.

Course Three: Leadership and Educational Change I

The third course, enrolling only mentor teachers, focused on developing the specific skills of an IC as they worked directly with a teacher candidate during the same semester. Teacher candidates began their internship experience with mentor teachers during the third week of the course, which provided an opportunity to create a warm and welcoming environment for teacher candidates. Teacher candidates wrote introductory biographies, which they shared with their mentor teachers. An in-depth analysis of the Danielson framework served as the foundation of the course as well as various methods of coaching/mentoring. Several in-class workshops focused on questioning and listening skills as well.

The course was derived from a variety of sources (Aguilar, 2013; Knight, 2007; Marzano & Simms, 2013; Yost et al., 2010). It focused on a sequence of collaborations between mentor teacher and teacher candidate concentrated on planning, teaching, reflecting, and applying new skills to encourage teacher mentors to work with their teacher candidate to develop instructional and management skills. Mentor teachers were encouraged to use active listening and Socratic questioning as they engaged with their teacher candidates. Using Danielson as a guide, mentor teachers began with building trust and then cycled through three rounds of preconferencing, observations, and postconferencing, each focused on a different Danielson domain. The cycle ended with the development of mutual goals for future growth.

Course assignments focused on coaching/mentoring teacher candidates. Three inquiry projects centered on the following three domains and subcomponents in the Danielson framework: Planning and Preparation, Classroom Environment, and Instruction. For each inquiry project, mentor teachers were required to:

1. Review lesson plans with their teacher candidate
2. Observe the lesson using the Danielson framework
3. Engage in a postobservation conference
4. Collaboratively develop an individual growth plan with the teacher candidate
5. Schedule a follow-up conference to establish future goals

Submissions included completed Danielson rubrics and summaries of teacher candidate conferences. In addition, coaching journals focused on establishing trust, understanding coaching types, creating a personal coaching "manifesto," and reflecting on the coaching experience as well as contributing to their coaching portfolio based on course content. A final assignment, completed during the break before the final course, involved working with peers in the school who were also completing the IC endorsement to design and implement a school-wide needs assessment of teachers in their school for future PLC/PD sessions. Analysis of these data commenced in the final course in the IC program.

Course Four: Leadership and Educational Change II

The fourth course was a continuation of the prior course, designed to encourage mentor teachers to work as informal teacher leaders within their schools, which is the hallmark of the IC model (Aguilar, 2013; Knight, 2007). The course focused on planning and implementing PLCs and coaching another mentor teacher who would coach another teacher candidate during the clinical internship experience.

This train-the-trainer model facilitated the growth of coaching knowledge and skills to a new set of mentor teachers. The course began with the mentor teachers' collection and analysis of needs assessment data, which would influence the design and implementation of future school-based PLC sessions. Along with an analysis of these data, mentor teachers investigated the research on the form and function of PLCs.

Course assignments connected directly to the work of an IC. ICs worked collaboratively on a handbook for mentoring teachers, based on content learned in the first three courses. The book facilitated their ability to coach "new" mentor teachers who hosted a new group of teacher candidates. A coaching plan/timeline and coaching journals captured the essence of these sessions. Principals were required to sit in on a few of these conferences, write a short synopsis, and submit their summaries to course instructors.

Finally, mentor teachers were required to cooperatively plan, execute, and reflect upon a series of PLC and PD sessions at their school, based on the needs identified in the data. In all, coaching practices with teacher candidates were extended to coaching practices with in-service teachers, which helped build instructional leadership capacity at each school. An integral part of the coursework involved mentor teachers creating and leading PLCs in their schools. The following section describes that endeavor.

Professional Learning Communities

As described, PLCs were an integral part of GPIC to allow ICs to broaden their work as school leaders beyond the internship experiences through PD facilitated by interdisciplinary IHE faculty trained within the IC program. The project gathered data on each PLC, documenting both processes and outcomes.

Key Attributes of PLCs

Each PLC focused on site-specific needs, sustained over a period of several months and structured to promote active learning and teacher-to-teacher collaboration (Corcoran & Consortium for Policy Research in Education, 1995; Garet et al., 2001). The GPIC PLC structure was derived primarily from DuFour's work. Specifically, each GPIC PLC exemplified DuFour's characteristics of effective PLCs, including improving instructional practice to ensure students learn, promoting collaboration and professional dialogue to achieve a common goal, and focusing on data-driven results (DuFour, 2004; Dufour & Dufour, 2007; DuFour & Mattos, 2013).

PLC Tracking

The PLCs were a space for collective inquiry focused on improving instructional practice to promote student learning (DuFour & Mattos, 2013). Each PLC group submitted an action plan to IHE facilitators that outlined a topic for the PLC with a measurable goal related to improving student learning, a schedule for meetings, and a strategy to collect data on PLC successes. ICs used a meeting report template, developed by the project with input from principals, to summarize the work completed in each PLC session, record attendees, note activities, and document next steps. The action plan and meeting report templates helped ensure that the work in PLCs reflected the research on high-quality learning communities promoted by the GPIC project.

PLC Results

GPIC supported PLCs in 15 schools, with over 162 teachers and six faculty facilitators working together to implement new school-based PLCs or improve upon existing PLCs. Seventy-seven percent of survey respondents reported that they found the PLC work to be the most useful aspect of GPIC, second only to the IC courses. The success of the PLCs inspired the decision to extend PLC work beyond the required time frame for an additional nine months in 11 of the schools.

The majority of the original PLCs focused on improving student behavior and emotional health ($n = 7$). The remaining PLCs focused on improving student achievement in math or language arts ($n = 3$); using technology in the classroom ($n = 2$); improving instruction within a specific domain of the Danielson framework ($n = 2$); and implementing innovative instructional strategies, such as project-based learning ($n = 1$). Upon the completion of their PLC experience, participants were surveyed. They agreed that "caring relationships exist among staff and students that are built on trust and respect" and "a culture of trust and respect exists for taking risks" in their practice.

Respondents also agreed that staff "informally shared ideas and suggestions for improving student learning" and worked together, had collegial relationships, and collaboratively analyzed data to improve instruction. Observers of the meetings reported that PLCs provided teachers with autonomy and the necessary support and resources to improve instructional practice. In interviews, university-based teacher educators noted that participating in PLCs helped them become part of the school community.

By establishing PLCs, GPIC was able to institutionalize change at partner schools. For example, one supervisor noted how the behavior of the entire school improved because of the PLC's focus on positive behavioral interventions. Hipp et al. (2008) noted that "for change to impact learning, it must focus on instructional practice" (p. 192). Through PLCs, the GPIC program created the type of collaborative learning opportunities for teachers that can lead to improvements in instruction (Hipp et al., 2008). As a result of their work in PLCs, both mentor teachers operating as instructional coaches and university faculty took a step toward achieving the kind of "simultaneous renewal" that is essential to "mutually beneficial" collaborations (Bier et al., 2012).

Above all, the program developed a collaborative university–school learning community that recognized and respected teachers as professionals (Corcoran & Consortium for Policy Research in Education, 1995). Stoll et al. (2006) noted that establishing effective PLCs is a long process that requires extensive work on the part of schools, which often require external support. GPIC offered training and resources to facilitate PLC work, including access to university faculty, books and materials, and planning templates.

Through supervised coursework ahead of PLC implementation, both university and school faculty worked to develop collaborative, respectful relationships to facilitate meaningful discussions about teaching and learning and work toward a shared goal (Bier et al., 2012; Frey et al., 2006; Lefever-Davis et al., 2007). The following section summarizes major themes of the model based on participants' survey results.

Signature Practices Derived from the GPIC Model

Upon completion of their participation in GPIC, students in the IC program responded to a survey to determine which program practices they perceived as most relevant to their work. GPIC provided significant themes from the coursework and asked respondents the extent to which their practice had changed and how much of that change was attributable to GPIC. Table 3.2, which highlights results of the data analysis, revealed six signature practices in their order of importance.

Table 3.2. Signature Practices

Signature Practice	Definition
Establishing Relationships	The ability to (1) establish trusting and mutually respectful relationships with colleagues and/or teacher candidates and (2) work effectively with people of different personality types, styles, and temperaments.
Coaching Teacher Candidates and Novice Teachers	The ability to (1) take on a leadership role with colleagues and (2) take on a coaching role with teacher candidates and/or novice teachers.
The Danielson Framework	(1) A deep understanding of the framework in relation to one's own teaching practice and (2) the ability to coach others based on the framework.
Reflection and Implementing Best Practices	(1) The ability to reflect upon the practice of teaching and (2) the use of evidence-based teaching strategies.
PD/PLCs and the Culture of Achievement	(1) The use of PD and PLCs in grade-level teams and/or the school building and (2) the culture of achievement in the school.
Setting Goals and Using Data to Make Decisions	(1) The use of questioning and listening strategies, (2) the ability to establish goals and follow through with them in coaching and/or teaching, and (3) the ability to make decisions based on data.

Throughout the coursework and experiences, mentor teachers identified the importance of *establishing relationships* with teacher candidates. Survey results revealed that mentor teachers built strong relationships with their teacher candidates by removing judgments from the conversation, being an active listener, and continuously monitoring and working on the relationship. Many mentor teachers noted the importance of building trust as the foundation of a successful relationship.

This result confirms extensive data analyses of the positive dyad relationships between mentor teacher and teacher candidates in an earlier study (see Richardson et al., 2019). As well, participants noted an enhanced ability to understand the perspectives of their peers to foster trusting relationships. University-based teacher educators commented that completing coursework with principals and mentor teachers opened the door to enhanced relationships, which assisted them in their work with teacher candidates.

Survey respondents noted a substantial change in their ability to *effectively coach* teacher candidates and engage adult learners in their buildings as they increasingly took on leadership roles. Their awareness of the power of effective communication to deliver positive and constructive criticism, as well as the importance of assisting teacher candidates to reflect, set goals, and improve in areas of need, also increased. In addition, participants learned to self-regulate their actions during a conversation, and they became more adept at active listening and questioning techniques.

Participants reported a change in their understanding of the Danielson framework. Before joining GPIC, teachers' familiarity with the Danielson framework varied from little exposure to years of experience, but, by the end, all participants had gained an in-depth understanding of each component of the framework and specific teacher actions that provide evidence for each rating. Participants also learned how the domains relate to each other and ways to use the rubric in coaching conversations.

Participants learned to *reflect* on and implement best practices through their IC coursework and their mentoring of teacher candidates. Participants identified journaling and reflection using the Danielson framework to guide conversations as the primary means of enhancing reflection on deeper levels. One mentor teacher commented, "reflection is not a way to berate my teaching abilities. Instead, it is a way to enhance my teaching abilities."

Results regarding PLC teams revealed that participants became more aware of the goals set for the group, adept at meeting their goals, and intentional about data. Noted earlier was the tremendous impact that PLCs had on each participating school. Mentor teachers learned the power of PLCs in enacting change focused on student learning in their schools through their informal leadership.

Finally, participants described being more purposeful about *goal setting* and using data in decision-making, realizing both as powerful tools to have targeted conversations with teacher candidates and in PLCs with peers.

Conclusion

The GPIC model focused primarily on educating mentor teachers on instructional coaching/mentoring skills to influence positive teacher candidate outcomes. Data from across the project, of which a small portion is reported here, suggests that the GPIC program was positively received by all stakeholders. As well, the PLCs supported data-driven change and six signature practices, which defined the IC program and enabled mentor teachers to work more effectively with teacher candidates (Richardson et al., 2019).

The literature clearly shows that the student teaching experience is paramount in shaping novice teachers' beliefs, levels of confidence, and resiliency to remain on the job, and therefore teacher education programs should work to enhance that experience (He, 2009; Richardson et al., 2019). The model presented in this chapter produced mentor teachers who were able to engage with teacher candidates, using differential coaching techniques, and serve as informal leaders in their school environments.

As well, the model showed great promise in promoting positive relationships among university-based teacher educators, principals, mentor teachers, and teacher candidates as evidenced by extensive data analysis reported in some detail here and elsewhere (see Richardson et al., 2019). Noted earlier, the literature discusses how trusting relationships that developed during the internship experience led to an enhanced experience for both teacher candidates and mentor teachers (Greiman, 2007; Russell & Russel, 2011; Sayeski & Paulsen, 2012; Wanberg et al., 2003).

Through coursework and establishing PLCs in schools, there were numerous opportunities for collaboration between principals, university-based teacher educators, and teacher candidates. An analysis of focus group discussions at the conclusion of the coursework revealed that enhanced relationships among mentor teachers, university-based teacher educators, and principals occurred. Many university-based teacher educators also commented that this was the first time that they had had a true relationship with the principal and mentor teacher before beginning their supervisory work.

Further, the model engaged schools through the implementation of PLCs aimed at improving teaching/learning within the context of each participating school. The literature discusses the importance of PLCs as an effective method for in-service PD (DuFour & Mattos, 2013). These IC course-required PLC initiatives provided opportunities for mentor teachers to become informal leaders within their schools. Survey data revealed that the PLCs helped to develop caring and trusting relationships among staff and focused on improving student learning.

While this chapter is intended to show teacher educators that it is possible to positively influence mentor teachers in their work with teacher candidates, it also shows the many partnership possibilities that serve to mutually enhance both schools and teacher education programs. Focused relationships and collaboration are the key attributes to success in any partnership endeavor.

References

Aguilar, E. (2013). *The art of coaching: Effective strategies for school transformation*. San Francisco: Wiley.

American Association of Colleges for Teacher Education. (2018). *A pivot toward clinical practice, its lexicon, and the renewal of educator preparation: A report of the AACTE Clinical Practices Commission*. http://www.nysed.gov/common/nysed/files/cpc-aactecpcreport.pdf

Bier, M. L., Park, C., Horn, I., Campbell, S., Kazemi, E., Hintz, A., & Peck, C. (2012). Designs for simultaneous renewal in university public school partnerships: Hitting the "sweet spot." *Teacher Education Quarterly*, 39(3), 127–141.

Corcoran, T. B., & Consortium for Policy Research in Education. (1995). *Helping teachers teach well: Transforming professional development*. https://files.eric.ed.gov/fulltext/ED388619.pdf

Danielson, C. (2011). *The framework for teaching: Evaluation instrument*. http://www.loccsd.ca/~div15/wp-content/uploads/2015/09/2013-framework-for-teaching-evaluation-instrument.pdf

DuFour, R. (2004). What is a "professional learning community"? *Educational Leadership*, 61(8), 6–11.

DuFour, R., & DuFour, B. (2007). What might be: Open the door to a better future. *National Staff Development Council*, 28(3), 27–28.

DuFour, R., & Mattos, M. (2013). How do principals really improve schools? *Educational Leadership*, 70(7), 34–40.

Dyson, M. (2010). What might a person-centred model of teacher education look like in the 21st century? The transformism model of teacher education. *Journal of Transformative Education*, 8(1), 3–21.

Frey, B. B., Lohmeier, J. H., Lee, S. W., & Tollefson, N. (2006). Measuring collaboration among grant partners. *American Journal of Evaluation*, 27(3), 383–392.

Garet, M., Porter, A., Desimone, L., Birman, B., & Yoon, K. (2001). What makes professional development effective? Results from a national sample of teachers. *American Educational Research Journal, 38*(4), 915–945.

Greiman, B. C. (2007). Influence on mentoring on dyad satisfaction: Is there an agreement between matched pairs of novice teachers and their formal mentors? *Journal of Career and Technical Education, 23*(1), 153–166.

Hammerness, K., Darling-Hammond, L., Grossman, P., Rust, F., & Shulman, L. (2005). The design of teacher education programs. In L. Darling-Hammond & J. Bransford (Eds.), *Preparing teachers for a changing world: What teachers should learn and be able to do* (pp. 390–411). San Francisco: Jossey-Bass.

He, Y. (2009). Strength-based mentoring in pre-service teacher education: A literature review. *Mentoring and Tutoring: Partnership in Learning, 17*(3), 263–275.

Hipp, K. K., Huffman, J. B., Pankake, A. M., & Olivier, D. F. (2008). Sustaining professional learning communities: Case studies. *Journal of Educational Change, 9*(2), 173–195. http://dx.doi.org/10.1007/s10833-007-9060-8

Knight, J. (2007). *Instructional coaching: A partnership approach to improving instruction.* Thousand Oaks, CA: Corwin Press.

Lefever-Davis, S., Johnson, C., & Pearman, C. (2007). Two sides of a partnership: Egalitarianism and empowerment in school-university partnerships. *Journal of Educational Research, 100*(4), 204–210.

Marzano, R. J., & Simms, J. A. (2013). *Coaching classroom instruction.* Bloomington, IN: Marzano Resources.

National Collaborating Centre for Methods and Tools. (2008). Partnership evaluation: The Partnership Self-Assessment Tool. https://www.nccmt.ca/registry/resource/pdf/10.pdf

Richardson, G., Yost, D., Conway, T., Magagnosc, A., & Mellor, A. (2019). Using instructional coaching to support student teacher-cooperating teacher relationships. *Action in Teacher Education.* https://doi.org/10.1080/01626620.2019.1649744

Russell M. L., & Russell, J. A. (2011). Mentoring relationships: Cooperating teachers perspectives on mentoring student interns. *The Professional Educator, 31*(1), 1–21.

Sayeski K. L., & Paulsen, K. J. (2012). Student teacher evaluations of cooperating teachers as indices of effective mentoring. *Teacher Education Quarterly, 39*(2), 117–130.

Smith, E. R., & Avetisian, V. (2011). Learning to teach with two mentors: Revisiting the "two-worlds pitfall" in student teaching. *The Teacher Educator, 46*, 335–354.

Stoll, L., Bolam, R., McMahon, A., Wallace, M., & Thomas, S. (2006). Professional learning communities: A review of the literature. *Journal of Educational Change, 7*(4), 221–258.

Wanberg, C. R., Welsh, E. T., & Hezlett, S. A. (2003). Measuring research: A review and dynamic process model. *Research in Personnel and Human Resources Management, 22*, 39–124.

Wang, J., & Odell, S. J. (2002). Mentored learning to teach according to standards-based reforms: A critical review. *Review of Educational Research, 72*(3), 481-546.

Yost, D. S., Vogel, R., & Liang, L. (2010). Embedded teacher leadership: Support for a site-based model of professional development. *International Journal of Leadership in Education, 12*(4), 409–433.

CHAPTER FOUR

Enhancing Mentor Teachers' Experience, Effectiveness, and Engagement Through Professional Development and University Communication

Glenda L. Black and Anna-Liisa Mottonen

> I mentor teacher candidates because it's such a learning experience on both sides. I'm always willing to learn, I'm ready to learn, I'm wanting to learn. I want to be able to give back. I was obviously a teacher candidate and I messed up. I learned from my mistakes. I'll be honest, I doubt very much if I would attend any professional development for my role as MT. It's like pulling teeth to get teachers to go to professional development. In my opinion, teachers are actually the worst students. We're terrible students, and we have terrible attention and think we know everything already. I really can't see mentor teacher professional development happening.
>
> —Erin, mentor teacher, personal communication, May 25, 2016

Although Erin appreciates the learning she garners from mentoring teacher candidates in her classroom, she does not perceive herself or other teachers participating in mentor teacher professional development (PD). Teacher preparation programs (TPPs) across the country rely on classroom teachers, referred to as mentoring teachers (MTs), to welcome teacher candidates (TCs) into their classrooms and provide meaningful professional development experience for the TCs (Allen et al., 2017; Clarke et al., 2012). Even though MTs recognize their need for professional development (Merchant, 2019) and are considered a major constituent in the preparation of TCs (Clarke et al., 2012; Gardner, 2006), classroom teachers are not well prepared to assume the mentorship role.

Historically, MTs have not received formal training to prepare them for their role as teachers of teaching (Brett et al., 2018; Hall et al., 2008; Sparks & Brodeur, 1987; Tang & Choi, 2007). Often, teachers choose not to participate in mentoring professional development (PD) opportunities because they feel their teaching experience alone qualifies them for the mentorship role (Leshem, 2014). Norman (2011) points to the concern that MTs are "underestimating the guidance that novices need in learning to plan" and not providing the teacher candidates with the processes and skills they need to "engage in while planning for student learning" (p. 50).

Tomlinson (2019) reported MTs would benefit from improvements in how mentoring strategies are structured. Since TPPs rely on classroom teachers to mentor TCs, they need to be provided with PD and support (Hudson, 2013). Following their participation in PD, MTs recognized the complex nature of mentoring and were successful in modifying their mentoring style based on their enhanced understanding of their role in different situations (Ambrosetti, 2014). This chapter describes how one TPP responded to the challenge to improve PD opportunities and communication with MTs by asking the MTs their opinions and implementing their suggestions where possible.

Ontario Context

To assist in understanding the mechanisms necessary to enhance support for MTs, the research was contextualized in Ontario, Canada, classrooms. In the teacher preparation program of study, TCs are admitted based on their undergraduate degree grades. Clinical practice takes place in Ontario classrooms during each of the four academic semesters (over two years) of the TPP. On completion of the TPP, TCs earn a Bachelor of Education degree.

The TPPs are accredited by the Ontario College of Teachers (OCT). To fulfill OCT program requirements, TCs must complete a minimum of 80 days of clinical practice in a publicly funded Ontario classroom. In the TPP of study, TCs complete 19 weeks (95 days) of clinical practice: 8 weeks in year one and 11 weeks in year two. Aside from a one-week placement, the first week of school, the clinical practice weeks are clustered into three six-week blocks.

To provide unique teaching experiences for the TCs, in year two, TCs complete a 60-hour Community Leadership Experience (CLE) within a four-week block. The CLE may include international or national fieldwork experience (i.e., Kenya, Costa Rica, France, Trois Pistoles, Quebec, or First Nation's schools) or with regional organizations (e.g., museums, outdoor education centers, correction centers) arranged by the TPP.

A mentor teacher is an experienced, qualified teacher who assumes the mentorship role for TCs for several weeks of clinical practice. Aside from the MT, TCs are also under the guidance of a university-based teacher educator (identified as faculty advisor in the TPP) who observes, supports, and evaluates the TC. Most university-based teacher educators are former school or district administrators (i.e., vice principals, principals, or superintendents) and act as a liaison between the university and the MT.

TPPs across the province recruit thousands of MTs to host TCs. To provide TCs with the opportunity to teach in the school district they wish to be employed or close to their home, the TPP accommodates these needs by offering clinical placements in 52 of 66 Ontario school districts. Clinical placement across the province creates a challenge for the university and the MTs to connect. Although the focus of this study was MTs, university-based educators have the same access to TPP support as MTs.

To better understand how to support MTs, current and former MTs were invited to participate in an online survey and semistructured interview to share their perspective on the types of support and format of delivery for PD. MTs make choices about their PD and participation in TCs' clinical practice. Self-determination theory provides a lens for understanding the motivating factors that influence their choices.

Theoretical Framework

To understand how to best support MTs, it is potentially useful to understand what drives their decision to mentor in the first place. An empirically based theory, "self-determination theory [identifies] three psychological needs—competence, relatedness, and autonomy—[that] are considered essential for understanding the what (i.e., content) and why (i.e., process) of goal pursuits" (Deci & Ryan, 2000, p. 229) and distinguishes between intrinsic and extrinsic motivation in terms of those psychological needs (Deci & Ryan, 2000; Ryan & Deci, 2000).

Intrinsic motivation involves engaging in an activity for its own sake (inherent satisfaction), while participating in an activity for an outcome separate from the activity (instrumental value) describes extrinsic motivation (Deci & Ryan, 2000). According to SDT, intrinsic motivation is superior to extrinsic motivation largely because it is more sustainable long term (Deci & Ryan, 2000; Ryan & Deci, 2000).

To relate SDT and intrinsic motivation to MTs specifically, intrinsic motivation to mentor TCs would involve mentoring for the enjoyment of the role itself, which would obviously be preferable, whereas examples of external motivators potentially driving teachers are administrative rewards or pressure for assuming mentorship (e.g., mentorship role is part of the job) (Niemiec & Ryan, 2009).

To promote intrinsic motivation to mentor TCs, the three psychological needs proposed by SDT—competence, relatedness, and autonomy—should be addressed among MTs. Teaching competence is described as a characteristic of efficiency, capability, or success in the classroom. For MTs, relatedness likely involves caring for their students and counseling their TCs on how to improve student achievement (Stanton, 2011).

If teachers make their own decisions (Ryan, 1995) about their mentorship practices, autonomy would be reportedly high. However, external control of these behaviors, imposed assignment of mentorship role, for example, is reported to impair autonomy and thereby intrinsic motivation (Deci & Moller, 2005; Niemiec & Ryan, 2009).

Despite limited research related to SDT and the MTs' motivation phenomena in the mentorship role, a case study by Eby et al. (2006) demonstrated findings consistent with SDT. Their examination of mentors' and protégés' perceptions of support for mentors and the mentoring outcomes revealed that the organizations' support for the mentors correlated positively with mentorship program outcomes.

Research suggests that, by fostering the components of self-determination, which include autonomy, relatedness, and competence, mentoring may have the potential to make work more meaningful and thereby enhance its potential to be intrinsically fulfilling (Kennett & Lomas, 2015).

Purpose of the Study

The purpose of this study was to understand how the current TPP could enhance teacher candidates' clinical practice by improving support and communication with MTs. More specifically, the research was guided by the following central questions: (1) What types of professional development and support do mentor teachers perceive as most beneficial for their role? (2) How can a TPP strengthen the connection between the university and clinical practice?

Method

A concurrent embedded strategy was employed for this mixed methods study (Greene, 2007, 2008); both types of data were collected simultaneously, with the qualitative (secondary) data embedded within the quantitative (primary) data. Participants completed a 40-item online survey, with questions related to the mentorship experience, relationship and communication with TC, mentorship skills, and supports for PD.

With the exception of the demographic questions, the statements were a combination of a five-point Likert scale ranging from most useful to least useful and space for additional comments. The last statement on the survey invited participation to an individual interview. A diverse group of 13 MTs were individually interviewed (Seidman, 2006, 2012) with a semistructured approach (Fontana & Frey, 2000) using a set of guiding questions to clarify and extend the discussion of supports for MTs.

Participants

Qualitative inquiry seeks to understand the meaning of a phenomenon from the perspectives of the participants; therefore, "it is important to select a sample from which the most can be learned" (Merriam, 2002, p. 12). All participants were elementary and secondary teachers in Ontario publicly funded schools. MTs from the TPP of study were invited to participate. A convenience sample of 281 MTs of varying ages and experience were drawn from 14 school districts representing North, South, Eastern, and Western regions of the province that included Catholic and non-Catholic publicly funded school districts, small and large schools, rural and urban schools, and schools with low- and high-socioeconomic status. The school districts that collaborate with the TPP reflect the diversity of Ontario teachers. Of the 281 MTs, 73% had more than 11 years of teaching experience.

Data Analysis

Survey data were ranked using an ordinal scale (Ary et al., 2010). Further methods of analysis for the project included three streams of activity identified by Miles and Huberman (1994): data reduction, data display, and conclusion drawing/verification. Deriving categories and themes elicited conclusions addressing the major research questions with support from the various data displays. Verification involved constant comparison of data from the various sources (interviews, reflections, field notes) to test the trustworthiness of the results (Glaser & Strauss, 1967; Handsfield, 2006).

Findings

To set a foundation for the recommended PD, MTs reported, with examples, the necessary mentorship skills to enhance TCs' clinical practice: patience, strong communication skills, teaching expertise, and developing a positive relationship. MTs shared their motivation for mentoring. Pseudonyms are used for all participants.

Motivation for Mentoring

MTs' motivation for mentoring TCs was to develop their goal of lifelong learning in addition to providing extra help in their classroom to improve students' learning. MTs welcomed the opportunity "to reflect on why you do what you do and the way you do it. When you have a TC, you're forced to explain your thinking behind what you're doing and it ends up good for you too" (Drew, personal communication, June 19, 2016).

MTs appreciated the opportunity to teach and work with adult learners. Mentoring TCs is a way for MTs to give back to the profession. "I was a teacher candidate and I messed up. I learned from my mistakes and I wanted to give teacher candidates the same opportunity before they get hired. I think it's also a two-way street" (Erin, personal communication, May 25, 2016). The mentorship role is assumed to be a way of giving back.

Research Question 1: Professional Development and Support Most Beneficial

The 281 respondents were asked to rate PD, support, or information on several components relevant to the role of MTs, each from least useful (1) to most useful (5), as presented in figure 4.1. The TPP structure of the practicum was rated as most useful (121 or 43%); roles and responsibilities were selected as most useful by the second most respondents (82 or 29%); and the TPP's TC evaluation was selected as most useful by the third largest number of respondents (79 or 28%).

TPP program overview. MTs interviewed said they would benefit from an overview of the TPP's course schedule, including brief descriptions of courses. As Devon (personal communication, May 20, 2016) stated, "It would be nice to know what courses they have taken prior to coming to help me know the candidates' knowledge." Further, MTs want to ensure their expectations are in line with the TPP.

Sample evaluations and bank of comments. MTs repeatedly reported they appreciated the sample evaluations available in the handbook. Drew (personal communication, June 19, 2016) noted she used the samples when she started

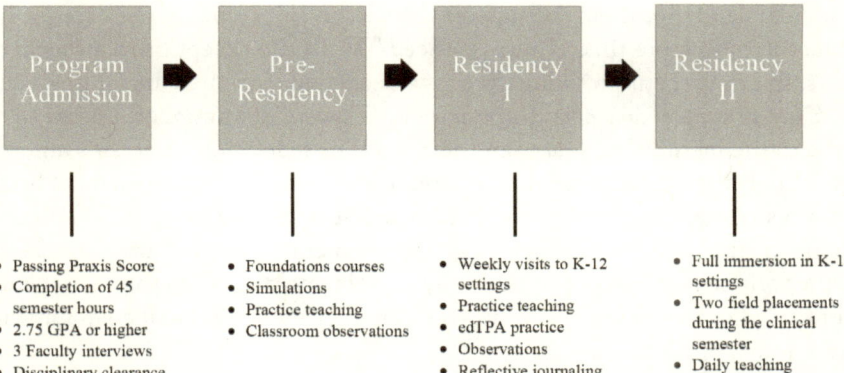

Figure 4.1.

mentoring TCs: "I needed some kind of sample to go by because it is different from assessing a young student in my class." Sample evaluations and a bank of comments for the evaluations would be helpful to writing the reports for the novice MTs.

Sample feedback for TCs having difficulties. MTs were comfortable providing positive feedback to the TCs. For some MTs, however, assistance in framing the difficult conversations for TCs would be appreciated. As Kim (personal communication, June 19, 2016) explains, "[I]t would be interesting to talk about how to give them feedback and phrasing on descriptive feedback. How would you tell a teacher candidate their attendance is an issue? Maybe I wasn't clear because she missed nine days."

Feedback from teacher candidates. Although not on the list of supports on the survey, requesting feedback from the teacher candidates was suggested by most of the associate teachers interviewed. Collective bargaining units (teacher unions) in Ontario prohibit TPPs from any sort of evaluation of associate teachers. Interestingly, MTs in their efforts to continue to improve their practice would appreciate feedback from teacher candidates. In Devon's (personal communication, May 20, 2016) words, "I think it would be awesome if there was some kind of feedback that we got on how the teacher candidates felt we did. What was helpful for them—that kind of thing."

Time. Although time was not included as one of the options for support on the survey, it was consistently noted as a factor that influenced mentor effectiveness. Morgan (personal communication, May 25, 2016) stated with emphasis, "Honestly, time! To really be able to give myself to the teacher candidate and give them the support they deserve, it comes at the expense of something, so more time is always a need." With the exception of struggling TCs, the time spent providing feedback decreased over the clinical practice.

Current support available. Interviewed MTs were not aware of support specific to the mentorship role from their teaching federation (teacher's union) or school district. Support at the school level was dependent upon school administrators. For some, participation was limited to arranging TC placements in the school with no further involvement or contact with the TCs. Other principals went out of their way to welcome the TC to the school and continued to "check on how things are going" (Devon, personal communication, May 20, 2016).

A few MTs felt empowered and a sense of autonomy by not having involvement from administration. In Erin's (personal communication, May 25, 2016) words, "[T]hey give me free rein. They ask me to open my classroom and do not tell me how to teach and what to offer my candidates."

Delivery methods for professional development. MTs suggested delivery models beyond the online option on the survey. A face-to-face workshop in their community was one option. They agreed that any face-to-face sessions should be delivered during the school day. The opportunity to meet with other MTs was appealing. Some MTs were reluctant to commit to any PD opportunities. In Alex's (personal communication, May 21, 2016) words, "I think it would depend on when that happens and what that training would entail."

She went on to explain the timing of the training would be an issue, "I'm just trying to think. When the year starts going, everything gets so crazy busy with programming, extra-curricular, and all of those things. And there are a lot of PD opportunities so it would depend on what their goals are." Some MTs admitted they were highly unlikely to participate in any training.

Research Question 2: Strengthen Connection between University and Clinical Practice

Among the 281 survey participants', email was rated as the most useful platform for TPPs to communicate (85 or 30%), followed by print (77 or 27%), and video (58 or 21%). The MTs interviewed preferred email as the most effective method of communication from the TPP. Most MTs preferred a print copy of the TPP handbook that outlines roles, responsibilities, schedules, sample lesson plans, and sample evaluations. Although not as popular as other delivery methods, video was listed as a support MTs would access if available.

As Sydney (personal communication, May 19, 2016) described, "By far and away, of that list, the one I would have been more likely to use would be watching a video on YouTube compared with the other options that were provided because for me, that's a lot easier." Accessing the website was suggested, but navigating websites was a challenge for some MTs.

Although not on the list of delivery methods or support, most MTs interviewed emphasized TCs need to contact their MT in advance of the placement. Furthermore, the MTs recommended TCs share information about themselves before arrival, including where they are from, their teaching divisions, subject specialty, number of clinical practices completed, and what they hope to get out of the experience. Repeated suggestions for communication after placement centered around feedback from TCs following a placement was repeatedly noted in the conversation about suggested communication.

As Jamie explains, "I'd like feedback from the teacher candidates too. It would be neat to know as a mentor teacher what they needed more of" (personal communication, May 25, 2016). Understanding the TC's perspective on the experience may provide insight into how he could approach a similar situation differently. MTs repeatedly stated they wished to complement what the TCs were learning on campus. Providing the MTs with topics, concepts, and issues introduced at the university, they could support the learning in their classroom.

Discussion

Congruent with Tomlinson (2019), MTs perceive information and support related to the TPP structure and mentorship strategies as tremendously important. There was almost unanimous support for using email as the method of communication between the university and the mentors. Consistent with the literature (Valencia et al., 2009), teachers received little or no PD to support their role as MTs. This gap in mentor teacher PD is disappointing since MTs often express the need for PD to improve their skills (Merchant, 2019).

Teaching federations and school districts provided no support, and the school administration's support was limited to welcoming and occasionally observing the TC in the classroom. When asked if they would participate in PD through the university, the responses varied from not at all to depending on the type and delivery method to enthusiasm for the possibility of PD.

There was no agreement on the method of delivering the support. Some preferred web based, and others preferred print versions of information. With no PD offered by the school or district, and in agreement with Hudson (2013), the responsibility for MT PD falls to the TPP. Identifying and offering differentiated PD to meet the varied needs and learning styles of the MTs remains a challenge. The provision of additional support for MTs mentoring struggling TCs was a strong recommendation by Valeni and Vogrinc (2007), a similar finding in this study, particularly for novice mentors.

As an explanation for teachers' mentoring motivation phenomena, self-determination theory (Deci & Ryan, 2000) offered valuable insight for the actions of the teachers in this study. Comparable to Stanton (2011), the strongest component of their psychological needs was relatedness, as evidenced by the teachers' strong commitment to caring for the personal and PD of their protégés. Teacher autonomy was reportedly low when they were not consulted on their option to mentor candidates. MTs agreed effective communication skills and teaching expertise were essential for a positive mentor–protégé relationship.

Current TPP Professional Development, Support, and Communication for MTs

Although proximity of the mentor teachers to the university remains a challenge, the TPP continues to endeavor to provide support to enhance MTs' effectiveness in mentoring TCs.

Professional Development

Considering the recommendations from MTs, the TPP provides MTs with varied PD and communication opportunities (online, print, and on campus). With the assistance of the university's technology support, a webpage dedicated to MT PD was created. The associate dean is responsible for managing the webpage with support from the clinical placement office staff. A link to the webpage is included in all email and print correspondence to the MTs. The webpage includes a range of resources MTs can access.

A program overview. Course summaries and organization of the courses for the two-year/4-semester (postgraduate) TPP is posted on the webpage and provided in print in the handbook and mailed to the MTs' school site.

TC evaluations. Teachers new to the MT role appreciate the sample TC evaluations with comment banks available on the webpage and in the mentor teacher handbook. Examples for each overall achievement level scoring is provided: (1) meets expectations with excellence, (2) meets expectations, or (3) does not meet expectations.

Instructional videos. Another type of resource added to the webpage is instructional videos on the following topics: MT skills, welcoming a TC, setting expectations, feedback-ongoing, feedback-corrective, and guidance for planning and instruction. The video clips (three to four minutes long) are of current MTs in various school settings providing insight on the topic of focus. To develop the videos, personal requests were made to exemplary MTs to speak on specific topics—ensuring geographic regions and grade levels were represented in the video segments. A TPP faculty member videotaped the MT responses at their school location. The university's technology support formatted the videos to the university's branding criteria.

Annual on-campus PD sessions. These are provided during the school day for MTs who teach in the same region as the university. Arranging for teacher release time is always a challenge, but, with financial support from the school district and when possible the Ministry of Education, one or two MTs from each school are able to participate in an event organized by the associate dean, clinical placement office, and interested faculty.

For example, one event was organized using an *Ed Camp* delivery model (Swanson, 2014). The morning began with activities for the MTs to reflect on their own practices and network with MTs from the region. Next, MTs recorded on sticky notes topics, issues, or concerns related to their MT role. Event facilitators organized the responses into six themes. MTs selected the theme they most wished to discuss. Theme groups worked through guided questions for a specific time limit for each question. MTs were brought together, and each theme shared a summary of their group's discussion.

Support and Communication
- Considering MTs' preference for communication, the TPP mostly uses print and electronic communication (email, dedicated webpage, and print handbooks for MTs).
- In advance of clinical practice, TCs contact their assigned MT and forward a detailed *Teacher Candidate Profile*, which includes their education background, personal interests and/or skills outside education, and professional goals for the clinical experience. The goal is to facilitate the development of a positive mentoring relationship. The profiles are appreciated by MTs.
- Teacher preparation program provides email reminders at critical points during the clinical practice. Attached to the emails are links to the instructional videos on the webpage.
- Annual MT awards were created to recognize the excellence in mentor teaching. Nominations are accepted from TCs, principals, or university educators.
- Support is ongoing and communication is frequent from the clinical practice office administration, associate dean, and university educators.

- Aside from the stipend, for each week they host a TC, MTs may accumulate credits toward a tuition voucher for a qualification course at the university.

Conclusion

Mentor teachers assume a major role in defining clinical practice and have a profound influence on the TCs' perceived self-efficacy (Allen et al., 2017; Black, 2015; Chambers, 2003; Saffold, 2005). However, most classroom teachers are unprepared to assume the mentorship role in the mentor/protégé relationship. Further, the literature underscores how MTs perceive the university–school interface to be fragmented, as evidenced in the disconnected roles of the university and clinical practice in TPPs (Bullough & Draper, 2004; Clarke & Collins, 2007).

This chapter provided insight into a TPP's study to understand how they could enhance support and communication for MTs in a geographic region that covers 52 school districts. Analysis of the results from the survey and semistructured interviews revealed that a one-size-fits-all was not going to work for MTs. Teachers' engagement for support was dependent on their experience as an MT or if they had a negative experience mentoring a TC. The type of communication from the TPP varied along a range of electronic to print correspondence delivered in the mail.

Although we continue to endeavor to explore avenues to support MTs who host teacher candidates, what was consistent in the results was the lack of support for MTs outside the TPP. A potential next step for the TPP is a collective opportunity for mentor teachers' PD, whereby school districts and bargaining units (teacher unions) could partner with the TPP to provide MT support and PD. School administrators could facilitate time at the beginning of a placement for the MT and TC to meet. The Ontario Ministry of Education allocates new teacher induction program funds. At the discretion of the principal or school district, these funds could be used for mentor teacher and teacher candidate *time*.

References

Allen, J. M., White, S., & Sim, C. (2017). Project evidence: Responding to the change professional learning needs of mentors in initial teacher education. *Australian Journal of Teacher Education*, 42(7), 14–25.

Ambrosetti, A. (2014). Are you ready to be a mentor? Preparing teachers for mentoring pre-service teachers. *Australian Journal of Teacher Education*, 39(6), 29–42.

Ary, D., Jacobs, L. C., & Sorensen, C. (2010). *Introduction to research in education* (8th ed.). Belmont, CA: Thomson Wadsworth.

Black, G. L. (2015). Developing teacher candidates' self-efficacy through reflection and supervising teacher support. *In-Education, 21*(1), 93–113.

Brett, P. D., Fizallen, N., Kilpatrick, S., Morrison, C., Reynolds, B., Kertesz, J., Quentin-Baxter, M., & Mansbridge, C. (2018). Learning the words: Supervising teachers and the language of impact in an initial teacher education programme. *Australian Journal of Teacher Education, 43*(8), 105–122.

Bullough, R. V. Jr., & Draper, R. J. (2004). Making sense of a failed triad: Mentors, university supervisors, and positioning theory. *Journal of Teacher Education, 55*, 407–420.

Chambers, S. (2003). The impact of length of student teaching on the self-efficacy and classroom orientation of pre-service teachers. Paper presented at the Annual Meeting of the Southwest Education Research Association, San Antonio, TX, ERIC document reproduction service No: ED 477 509.

Clarke, A., & Collins, S. (2007). Complexity science and student teacher supervision. *Teaching and Teacher Education, 23*(2), 160–172.

Clarke, A., Collins, J., Triggs, V., Nielsen, W., Augustine, A., Coulter, D., & Weil, F. (2012). The mentoring profile inventory: An online resource for cooperating teachers. *Teaching Education, 23*(2), 167–194.

Deci, E. L., & Moller, A. C. (2005). The concept of competence: A starting place for understanding intrinsic motivation and self-determined extrinsic motivation. In A. J. Elliot & C. J. Dweck (Eds.), *Handbook of competence and motivation* (pp. 579–597). New York: Guilford Press.

Deci, E. L., & Ryan, R. M. (2000). The "what" and "why" of goal pursuits: Human needs and the self-determination of behavior. *Psychological Inquiry, 11*(4), 227–268.

Eby, T. L., Lockwood, A. L., & Butts, M. (2006). Perceived support for mentoring: A multiple perspectives approach. *Journal of Vocational Behavior, 68*, 267–291.

Fontana, A., & Frey, J. H. (2000). The interview: From structured questions to negotiated text. In N. K. Denzin & Y. S. Linson (Eds.), *Handbook of qualitative research* (2nd ed.; pp. 649–656). Thousand Oaks, CA: Sage.

Gardner, S. (2006). Producing well-prepared teachers. *Education Digest, 71*(6), 42–46.

Glaser, B., & Strauss, A. (1967). *The discovery of grounded theory: Strategies for qualitative research*. Chicago, IL: Aldine.

Greene, J. C. (2007). *Mixed methods in social inquiry*. San Francisco: John Wiley.

Greene, J. C. (2008). Is mixed methods social inquiry a distinctive methodology? *Journal of Mixed Methods Research, 2*(1), 7–22.

Hall, K. M., Draper, R. J., Smith, L. K., & Bullough, R. V. (2008). More than a place to teach: Exploring the perceptions of the roles and responsibilities of mentor teachers. *Mentoring and Tutoring: Partnerships in Learning, 16*(3), 328–345.

Handsfield, L. (2006). Being and becoming American: Triangulating habitus, field, and literacy instruction in a multilingual classroom. *Language & Literacy, 8*(3), 1–26.

Hudson, P. (2013). Mentoring as professional development: Growth for both mentor and mentee. *Professional Development in Education, 39*(5), 771–783.

Kennett, P., & Lomas, T. (2015). Making meaning through mentoring: Mentors finding fulfilment at work through self-determination and self-reflection. *International Journal of Evidence Based Coaching and Mentoring, 13*(2), 29–44.

Leshem, S. (2014). How do teacher mentors perceive their role, does it matter? *Asia-Pacific Journal of Teacher Education, 4*(3), 261–274.

Merchant, H. (2019). *Becoming mentors: Mentor praxis and self-directed development* (Doctoral dissertation, Middle and Secondary Education Dissertations).

Merriam, S. (2002). *Qualitative research in practice: Examples for discussion and analysis.* San Francisco: Jossey-Bass.

Miles, M. B., & Huberman, A. M. (1994). *Qualitative data analysis* (2nd ed.). Thousand Oaks, CA: Sage.

Niemiec, C. P., & Ryan, R. M. (2009). Autonomy, competence, and relatedness in the classroom: Applying self-determination theory to educational practice. *Theory and Research in Education, 7*(2), 133–144.

Norman, P. J. (2011). Planning for what kind of teaching? Supporting cooperating teachers as teachers of planning. *Teacher Education Quarterly, 38*(3), 49–68.

Ryan, R. M. (1995). Psychological needs and the facilitation of integrative processes. *Journal of Personality, 63*(3), 397–427.

Ryan, R. M., & Deci, E. L. (2000). Intrinsic and extrinsic motivations: Classic definitions and new directions. *Contemporary Educational Psychology, 25*(1), 54–67.

Saffold, F. (2005). Increasing self-efficacy through mentoring. *Academic Exchange Quarterly, 9*(4), 13–16.

Seidman, I. (2006). *Interviewing as qualitative research: A guide for researchers in education and the social sciences* (3rd ed.). New York: Teachers College Press.

Seidman, I. (2012). *Interviewing as qualitative research: A guide for researchers in education and the social sciences* (4th ed.). New York: Teachers College Press.

Sparks, S., & Brodeur, D. (1987). Orientation and compensation for cooperating teachers. *The Teacher Educator, 23*(1), 2–12.

Stanton, K. C. (2011). *Engineering faculty motivation for and engagement in formative assessment* (Unpublished doctoral dissertation). Virginia Polytechnic Institute and State University, Blacksburg, VA.

Swanson, K. (2014). Edcamp: Teachers take back professional development. *Educational Leadership, 71*(8), 36–40.

Tang, S. Y. F., & Choi, P. L. (2007). Connecting theory and practice in mentor preparation: Mentoring for the improvement of teaching and learning. *Mentoring and Tutoring: Partnership in Learning, 13*(3), 383–401.

Tomlinson, P. (2019). *Mentor teachers' perceptions of effective mentoring strategies* (Doctoral dissertation, Walden Dissertations and Doctoral Studies).

Valencia, S. W., Martin, S. D., Place, N. A., & Grossman, P. (2009). Complex interactions in student teaching: Lost opportunities for learning. *Journal of Teacher Education, 60*(3), 304–322.

Valeni, M., & Vogrinc, J. (2007). A mentor's aid in developing the competencies of teacher trainees. *Educational Studies, 33*(4), 373–384.

CHAPTER FIVE

Mentor Study Groups as Sites for Mentor Teacher Learning

Amy R. Guenther, Lindsay J. Wexler, Susan K. Brondyk, Randi N. Stanulis, and Stacey Pylman

> Up to this point, we have never been taught how to mentor a person. Seriously! You can be a great teacher and a horrible mentor. [It's assumed] that if you know how to teach, then you will just know how to [mentor] or figure it out.
>
> —Travis, Mentor Teacher, Grade 4

Mentor teachers (MTs) are one of the most influential aspects of teacher preparation (Clarke et al., 2014; Grossman, 2010; Morin, 1993), playing a key role in the student teaching experience. Yet far too many MTs lack the preparation that enables them to provide high-quality support for teacher candidates (TCs) (Clarke et al., 2014). As Travis suggests, teaching skills do not necessarily equate to mentoring skills, and MTs are often left to "figure out" how to mentor on their own.

Even for those MTs who do receive some type of support, not all of these experiences are equal, as some are more growth-producing or "educative" than others. While researchers have identified the skills, knowledge, and dispositions of MTs who provide educative experiences for novice teachers (e.g., Clarke et al., 2014; Feiman-Nemser, 1998, 2001a, 2001b; Stanulis & Floden, 2009), far less has been written about the ways in which MTs develop an educative stance and practice. Without intentional support and experiences, MTs are less likely to develop and enact the type of educative practices that will maximize learning for TCs.

We contend the process of becoming an educative mentor is connected to being part of a particular kind of learning community. This chapter describes a specific model of professional learning for MTs referred to as Mentor Study Groups (MSGs). These inquiry-based communities are collaborative partnerships where MTs and university-based teacher educators inquire into their mentoring practice, in much the same way they will inquire about teaching with their mentees.

Situating Mentor Study Groups

MSGs are based upon a particular vision of learning and grounded in related theories. They are conceptually based on Dewey's (1938) notion of educative experiences. From his observations of children, Dewey discovered some learning experiences propel learners forward more than others, particularly those that build upon previous experiences and prepare the learner for future learning. This happens when the movement toward a goal is mediated by an interaction with another and together the participants make meaning from the experience.

Expanding on these ideas, Feiman-Nemser (2001a) conceptualized "educative mentoring," which fosters growth-producing experiences that help novices "continue learning in and from their practice" (Feiman-Nemser, 1998, p. 66). Educative mentors explain why and how they do something, situate experiences within the complexity of practice, acknowledge themselves as lifelong learners, and value contributions from their TCs and encourage them to have a voice (Feiman-Nemser, 1998, 2001a; Stanulis & Bell, 2017; Stanulis et al., 2014).

Underlying the design of MSGs is the belief that learning occurs through social interaction (among MTs as well as between MT and TC), rather than in isolation (Lave, 1996; Putnam & Borko, 2000). Specifically, this work draws on one such social learning theory, the theory of assisted performance, which explains how, with assistance from a more experienced person, a learner can "engage in levels of activity that could not be managed alone" (Tharp & Gallimore, 1988, p. 28). The process of assisted performance includes identifying performance levels, structuring situations, scaffolding support, and preparing for unassisted performance (Stanulis et al., 2014). Thus, MTs' current knowledge we utilize while providing the support they need to gradually take on educative mentoring practices themselves. Learning opportunities we create in which new learning is scaffolded and, at the same time, model the type of "teaching" that MTs will do with their TCs.

We also utilize Timperley's (2011) concept of professional learning, which describes the "internal process in which individuals create professional knowledge through interaction with this information in a way that challenges previous assumptions and creates new meaning" (p. 5). Thus, MSGs we structure as places where MTs experience familiar practices, such as co-planning and analysis of student work, in new ways and are supported as they learn to enact them. Based on these ideas, MSGs are intentionally designed as sites for collaborative learning in which participants help define and internalize the practices of mentoring through observation, analysis, and discourse (Dewey, 1938; Lave & Wenger, 1991).

Mentor Study Groups in Action

Although the focus of this chapter is on mentoring TCs, it is important to note the MSG model can be utilized in multiple contexts. The model presented here, for instance, is predicated on prior induction work in urban districts where both administrators and induction mentors were supported in their work with beginning teachers during their first three years of teaching (Stanulis & Brondyk, 2013; Stanulis & Floden, 2009; Stanulis et al., 2014). Sessions for school administrators helped them to understand the importance of and create cultures to support beginning teacher learning (e.g., selection of educative MTs and release time for MTs). Monthly meetings (both virtual and in person) with induction MTs provided them with the knowledge and tools to assist beginning teachers to enact high-leverage practices, such as discussion-based teaching, that they might not otherwise be able to implement on their own. In some districts MTs were also equipped to facilitate professional learning communities, in which beginning teachers and MTs alike examined their teaching practices. This work laid the foundation for teaching and supporting educative mentoring and, thus, served as a structure for the teacher preparation–based MSGs described in this chapter.

For our teacher preparation–based MSGs, we create learning opportunities were created where mentors of TCs—the school-based MTs and university-based teacher educators who serve as university supervisors—come together for collaborative talk and reflection. Because a key component of MSGs is regular time together with enough time for conversation and practice, the MSGs occur six times over the course of the school year in the MTs' schools for 90-minute sessions with a university-based teacher educator facilitating the meeting. The typical structure of the MSG includes time for MTs and university-based teacher educators (including the facilitator and university supervisor) to reflect on and analyze their mentoring practice and learn about educative mentoring practices. We describe this process of ongoing, scaffolded support and joint inquiry in the following subsections.

Ongoing, Scaffolded Support
Learning to mentor educatively requires ongoing scaffolding that meets MTs where they are and is growth-producing for all participants. At the beginning of study group time, participants need opportunities to differentiate between traditional and educative mentoring. Traditional mentoring focuses on immediate concerns and fixing problems, providing advice and suggestions, and telling rather than asking (Bradbury, 2010). Teachers who mentor in this more traditional way work to be helpful by sharing resources, providing tips, and solving problems.

MSG participants talk about the limits of this as the primary approach to helping someone learn. Rather than telling and providing solutions, educative mentoring encourages MTs to think about the questions, dispositions, and long-term orientations of teaching that we hope to foster in novice teachers. The development of an educative mentoring stance requires MSGs that are designed as a series of connected learning experiences, thus the multiple sessions over the course of the school year. These learning opportunities allow for observation, analysis, and rehearsal of practices, during which participants model risk-taking and work together to build a new conception of mentoring.

The typical structure of an MSG includes time for MTs and university-based teacher educators to analyze their mentoring practices based on a shared image of good teaching that the teachers are mentoring toward, while learning about one of three educative mentoring practices: co-planning, observing and debriefing, and analyzing student work (Stanulis et al., 2019). In early sessions, MTs watch or listen to examples of one of the educative mentoring practices, while the facilitator identifies the educative mentoring moves. Then, participants talk together about various ways to implement the practice with their novices. For example, when learning about observing and debriefing, MTs watch a video of classroom instruction, practice gathering evidence from observation, and discuss ways to create notes from this data to engage in a debriefing conversation with their TC.

This scaffolded practice provides MTs with the opportunity to try out tools and conversation techniques before debriefing with their TC. MTs then try out the practice, audio-record the conversation with their TC, and reflect on their mentoring. At the next MSG session, the MTs share their records of practice (e.g., audio and video recordings) and reflections, analyzing what happened when they tried the mentoring practice under discussion.

These records of practice are utilized to highlight MTs' actual voices by playing samples of MTs' recorded conversations in the MSG. The MTs then discuss educative attributes they hear and make note of mentoring moves. In future sessions, they repeat this cycle with other mentoring practices. The MSG model is designed to cycle through the three educative mentoring practices twice each year, with the second time building on the previous experiences of the group.

Sharing records of practice provides opportunities for reflection and discussion that can propel the MTs forward toward independence as they continue the cycle of implementation, reflection, and feedback. This sharing also provides facilitators with information about each MT as a learner. In each MSG, university facilitators use talk moves associated with scaffolded assistance. These talk moves include voicing instructional moves, questioning, and unpacking thinking (Tharp & Gallimore, 1988; Ball & Cohen, 1999; Tomlinson, 1999).

Unpacking thinking is a particularly important element of educative mentoring, as it provides learners access to a more knowledgeable person's thought process so that they can begin to understand the reasoning behind actions. During MSGs, facilitators model thinking aloud in hopes that MTs will share their reasoning with TCs in much the same way. MTs also model their own thinking aloud as they gain confidence and skill. Role-playing activities provide MTs with opportunities to practice thinking aloud before trying it out in the field.

Scaffolding is critical to learning in MSGs. Scaffolding allows MTs to enact small elements of a practice with the assistance of an experienced facilitator, who "controls those elements of the task that are initially beyond the learner's capability, thus permitting him to concentrate upon and complete only those elements that are within range of his competence" (Wood et al., 1976, p. 90). Learning is an iterative series of trials, reflection, and adjustment. Scaffolded learning involves introducing small, manageable chunks of a larger practice, which are discussed, modeled, practiced, and analyzed as needed. Throughout this process, the MSG facilitators make continual adjustments and are "responsive" to the learner's level of performance and changing needs (Tharpe & Gallimore, 1988, p. 40). Through this assisted performance, the MTs are able to enact educative practices that they would not otherwise be able to without support.

Joint Inquiry

Perhaps the most constructive feature of MSGs is the joint inquiry that occurs among the participants. Within MSGs, the process of becoming an educative MT is connected to being part of a particular kind of learning community, as being a learner is a key feature of educative mentoring. On a monthly basis, MSGs provide opportunities for MTs and university-based teacher educators to genuinely inquire into teaching, using data such as the MTs' records of practice and student work samples as a basis for their conversations. The heart of this type of inquiry is that all voices are valued. Facilitators bring their expertise to the conversation but do not hold all of the knowledge. Input from MTs is vital to the discussion because they can contribute information about the context, mentee, and their own experiences.

In this way, the power dynamics shift from the facilitator having all the answers to a dialogue in which participants contribute to the learning of others. The facilitator, as one member of this community, not only assists the MTs in their journey to become more educative but also develops their own teaching practice along the way. These types of conversations require all members to risk some level of vulnerability as they open up their practice to the group. The benefit, however, is that, as trust grows, organic questions and issues often arise that lead to authentic exploration of effective teaching and through this process, MTs get to experience the types of conversations that facilitators hope they will have with their TCs.

Learning through Mentor Study Groups

We piloted, and simultaneously studied, the aforementioned MSGs in an elementary teacher preparation program that culminates in a yearlong student teaching experience. A subset of the larger university-based program, participants included 23 MTs who had previously hosted TCs for student teaching, six university-based teacher educators who served as university supervisors, and two university-based teacher educators who served as facilitators. MTs and university-based teacher educators were split among six MSGs, with each facilitator leading three MSGs.

As part of our study of the pilot, we collected recordings of monthly MSG sessions, MT/TC conversations that occurred as MTs engaged in the practice being studied, MT end-of-the-year interviews, and written reflections the MTs completed at each MSG. Through analysis of this data (see Stanulis et al. [2019] for methodology), we found the MSGs provided a community of learning in which participants helped define and internalize the practices of educative mentoring through observation, analysis, and discourse. As one MT explained,

> Listening to other people's videos or their conversations with their [TCs] . . . helped me think about things in a different perspective and of conversations I could have with my [TC]. I liked the idea that we had that community of people to meet with and talk to and bounce ideas off of each other.

Through the support of MSGs, MTs began to develop skills needed to enact the core mentoring practices of co-planning, observing and debriefing, and analyzing student work in educative ways. Concurrently, they began to see their role as teacher educators more than as merely supervisors or cheerleaders (Stanulis et al., 2019). In the words of another MT as she compared her mentoring experience before MSGs and after,

> I feel like last year as a mentor teacher I was probably more of a . . . cheerleader. . . . I know I did her such an injustice because I'm looking now at some things that we do here [together in the mentor study groups] . . . and just the whole explaining why I'm doing what I'm doing . . . [now] she's grown so much.

Through the professional learning opportunities the MSGs provided, MTs developed skills to examine and articulate complex practices of teaching with their TCs (Stanulis et al., 2019). Though the MSG facilitators presented each practice to the MTs initially, through the process of trying them out, reflecting on conversations with their TCs, and sharing across the group, they were able to make the practices their own. Stanulis et al. (2019) defined the core mentoring practices in the words of the MTs, as it is the MTs' experiences that shaped our understanding of what educative co-planning, observing and debriefing, and analyzing student work look like in practice. The practices shifted throughout the year; through enactment and analysis of each practice in the first cycle, they were jointly able to set goals to further enrich the practices during the second cycle of enactment as the TCs took the lead in teaching. Through the support of MSGs, MTs became more focused in their mentoring, enacted the core practices with higher frequency and across curricula, and worked specifically to make their thinking visible to the TC. Reflecting in writing, one MT noted,

> Focusing in on one teaching strategy was easier/more effective than trying to comment on everything. I feel like [TC] and I had a richer discussion and could analyze data knowing that we were focused on one aspect of the lesson. It allowed for deeper discussion instead of a broader commentary.

Helping MTs focus their mentoring efforts led to "richer" discussions, which had implications for TC learning (Wexler, 2020).

Finally, as MTs became more skillful at enactment, they began to blur core practices, meaning that in single conversations MTs drew on multiple core practices to enrich the learning opportunity for TCs. For example, discussions between MTs and TCs that began as focused debriefing conversations turned into analyses of student work. In other cases, analyzing student work led into co-planning conversations. In one instance, after looking at the variety of student responses on a class assignment, one MT asked her TC to pull students into small groups for targeted reinforcement. She said,

> What I would like to do now with these few kids, there's like three in each one of these two groups that made similar errors . . . either during DEAR time or during morning work time, is just pulling them to the back table.

This excerpt illustrates how the MT used analyzing student work as a natural segue into co-planning. In these ways, it is evident that MTs became more educative in their work with TCs through the MSG process. Indeed, all participants shifted their practice in some way. The shifts in enactment of 10 focal participants are highlighted in Stanulis et al. (2019).

MSGs were designed and facilitated in deliberate ways. Selected core mentoring practices were clearly defined for MTs along with audio and video examples. MTs were given time to enact the practices, and then they returned to the MSG to share experiences, reflect, and set goals. As a result,

> Teachers shifted their thinking and came to view their role as that of an educative mentor. This shift happened as [the participating] teachers became intentional about the ways in which they enacted common mentoring practices. This shift was not accidental. With purposeful experiences, practice and reflection, educative mentoring was learned. (Stanulis et al., 2019, p. 12)

This purposefully designed model allowed university-based teacher educators, MTs, and TCs to grow and learn together.

Implementation Insights

To assist implementation efforts in other university-based programs, we offer some insights gained from our work with teacher preparation–based MSGs, including some of the challenges we faced during both the pilot and implementation phases throughout the elementary preparation program in subsequent years.

We begin with some additional information on logistics. For the pilot, MSGs were held in small groups of three to five teachers in their home schools. As we expanded to include all of the MTs in the elementary program, finite staffing (two university facilitators) necessitated combining teachers from multiple schools in the same district into larger MSGs of six to eight teachers. Based on further reduction in MSG facilitators due to budget cuts, the MSGs grew to eight to ten MTs and included teachers from neighboring districts.

These larger MSGs required more partner or trio work during the MSG sessions and fewer whole-group discussions to engage all of the MTs. Other than the first MSG session, which was part of a half-day professional development workshop for MTs held at the university prior to the start of the school year, MSG sessions occurred during the school day. These sessions began in October, once the MTs and university-based teacher educators agreed the TCs could successfully cover their classes for the duration of the MSG session. Notably, all TCs in this program enter student teaching having met the state requirements for substitute teaching.

Mentoring in educative ways necessitated a shift in thinking for many MTs and university supervisors. This shift was from a largely supervisory role that focused on providing advice and emotional support to the role of teacher educator, which focused on inquiry and growth (Stanulis et al., 2019). Thus, in the opening MSG session and throughout the year, it was important to convey the importance and potential of educative mentoring and show the MTs and university-based teacher educators how they could use their expertise to maximize TC learning.

Mentoring in educative ways required more time than a typical supervisory approach. Most MTs were able to enact the practices they learned in their MSGs by engaging in educative discussions with their TCs during their planning time over the course of the school day. However, some of the MTs did not have planning time during the school day due to budget cuts in their district. As a result, some of these MTs found it difficult to regularly implement the educative mentoring practices. The MTs, in one particular district, who did regularly implement the practices extended their workday without additional compensation.

In an effort to be responsive to the learners in our MSGs, we solicited feedback from them midway through and at the end of the academic year and made changes accordingly. For example, feedback from university-based teacher educators led us to use existing university supervisor monthly meetings to preview each mentoring practice and corresponding strategies prior to their MSG. Also, some technology challenges were addressed by eliminating the requirement for MSG members to upload the audio recordings of their practice-focused sessions. Lastly, based on feedback from a focus group of MTs and university-based teacher educators, which we convened over the summer, we condensed the materials and incorporated time for reflective writing within the MSG.

We initiated the pilot MSGs through the support of the department chair, who allocated funding for 20 hours per week for two graduate students (10 hours per student). These graduate students served as the MSG facilitators and assisted the director of the MSG program with curriculum design and research. Additional funding also afforded a reduced caseload for the university-based teacher educators who participated as university supervisors in the MSGs and assisted with research. In order to sustain the program after the primary pilot funding was exhausted, the field placement coordinator began taking on a professional development role, assisting with MSG implementation as a group facilitator.

Implications

This model of MT professional learning contributes to the collective understanding of innovative ways to utilize teachers' expertise to enhance their mentoring capabilities and ultimately support TCs and novice teachers. The framework presented in this chapter emphasizes the importance of collaborative inquiry and assisted performance in developing educative mentors for TCs. As Stanulis et al. (2019) contend,

> Just as learning to teach requires deliberate interactions with a knowledgeable other (Vygotsky, 1978), so too does learning to mentor. Just as planning and analyzing student work are complex teaching tasks that need to be learned (Kazemi & Franke, 2004; Norman, 2011), so too are the mentoring moves needed to facilitate the learning of these tasks. (p. 12)

Teacher preparation programs can facilitate communities of practice around mentoring where mentors' teaching expertise are maximized through the implementation of educative mentoring practices. They can provide professional learning experiences where MTs inquire into their mentoring practices with the support of their colleagues and university personnel. Together, they can work toward a type of mentoring that positively influences the TCs' growth both now and in the future.

Furthermore, MSGs provide opportunities for university-based teacher educators and their PK–12 partners to engage in conversations about teaching and learning in which both parties contribute ideas and work collaboratively. Unlike the typical unilateral decision-making that is so common in teacher education—where the program leaders inform their PK–12 placements of their vision and requirements—MSGs offer an example of a new way to work together with PK–12 partners. They give voice to MTs, as they are asked to jointly participate in conversations about mutually agreed upon expectations for TCs and shared accountability for TC outcomes. For instance, as MTs engage in the joint work, along with university-based teacher educators, of planning a post observation debriefing session and then analyzing a video clip of that actual conversation, they have the opportunity to talk about specific examples of effective teaching and to hear from one another about their respective understandings and experiences. PK–12 MTs are able to participate in shaping the learning experience for the novice while at the same time learning to become an educative mentor.

A deliberately designed and sustained MSG model can support MTs to develop into educative mentors. When MTs are supported through targeted, inquiry-based professional development, the mentoring practices they are able to enact with TCs change (Stanulis et al., 2019). The particular activities of mentoring that MTs use to support the TCs do make a difference (Wexler, 2020); when done in educative ways, co-planning, observing and debriefing, and analyzing student work support novice teacher learning (Stanulis et al., 2019).

Opportunities for MT professional learning matter for TC learning and influence the instructional practices they are able to implement while a student teacher and beginning teacher (Wexler, 2020). TCs who work with MTs supported through MSGs are likely to have experiences that allow them to think about and engage in complex facets of teaching as beginning teachers (Wexler, 2020). For these reasons, supporting MTs to enact educative mentoring practices through MSGs is essential.

References

Ball, D. L., & Cohen, D. K. (1999). Developing practice, developing practitioners: Toward a practice-based theory of professional education. In G. Sykes & L. Darling-Hammond (Eds.), *Teaching as the learning profession: Handbook of policy and practice* (pp. 3–32). San Francisco: Jossey Bass.

Bradbury, L. (2010). Educative mentoring: Promoting reform-based science teaching through mentoring relationships. *Science Education*, 94(6), 1049–1071.

Clarke, A., Triggs, V., & Nielsen, W. (2014). Cooperating teacher participation in teacher education: A review of the literature. *Review of Educational Research, 84*(2), 163–202.

Dewey, J. (1938/1997). *Education and experience*. New York: Simon & Schuster.

Feiman-Nemser, S. (1998). Teachers as teacher educators. *European Journal of Teacher Education, 21*(1), 63–74.

Feiman-Nemser, S. (2001a). From preparation to practice: Designing a continuum to strengthen and sustain teaching. *Teachers College Record, 103*(6), 1013–1055.

Feiman-Nemser, S. (2001b). Helping novices learn to teacher: Lessons from an exemplary support teacher. *Journal of Teacher Education, 52*(1), 17–30.

Grossman, P. (2010). *Learning to practice: The design of clinical experience in teacher preparation*. [Policy brief]. Partnership for Teacher Quality. https://www.nea.org/assets/docs/Clinical_Experience_-_Pam_Grossman.pdf

Kazemi, E., & Franke, M. L. (2004). Teacher learning in mathematics: Using student work to promote collective inquiry. *Journal of Mathematics Teacher Education, 7*(3), 203–235.

Lave, J. (1996). Teaching, as learning, in practice. *Mind, Culture, and Activity, 3*(3), 149–164.

Lave, J., & Wenger, E. (1991). *Situated learning: Legitimate peripheral participation*. New York: Cambridge University Press.

Morin, J. A. (1993). The effectiveness of field experiences as perceived by student teachers and supervising teachers. *Teacher Education Quarterly, 20*(4), 49–64.

Norman, P. J. (2011). Planning for what kind of teaching? Supporting cooperating teachers as teachers of planning. *Teacher Education Quarterly, 38*(3), 49–68.

Putnam, R. T., & Borko, H. (2000). What do new views of knowledge and thinking have to say about research on teacher learning? *Educational Researcher, 29*(1), 4–15.

Stanulis, R. N., & Bell, J. (2017). Beginning teachers improve with attentive and targeted mentoring. *Kappa Delta Pi Record, 53*(2), 59–65.

Stanulis, R. N., & Brondyk, S. K. (2013). Complexities involved in mentoring towards a high-leverage practice in the induction years. *Teachers College Record, 115*(10), 1–34.

Stanulis, R. N., Brondyk, S. K., Little, S., & Wibbens, E. (2014). Mentoring beginning teachers to enact discussion-based teaching. *Mentoring and Tutoring: Partnership in Learning, 22*(2), 127–145.

Stanulis, R. N., & Floden, R. E. (2009). Intensive mentoring as a way to help beginning teachers develop balanced instruction. *Journal of Teacher Education, 60*(2), 112–122.

Stanulis, R. N., Wexler, L. J., Pylman, S., Guenther, A., Farver, S., Ward, A., Croel Perrien, A., & White, K. (2019). Mentoring as more than "cheerleading": Looking at educative mentoring practices through mentors' eyes. *Journal of Teacher Education, 70*(5), 567–580.

Tharp, R. G., & Gallimore, R. (1988). *Rousing minds to life: Teaching, learning and schooling in social context.* New York: Cambridge University Press.

Timperley, H. (2011). *Realizing the power of professional learning.* McGraw-Hill Education (UK).

Tomlinson, C. A. (1999). Mapping a route toward differentiated instruction. *Educational Leadership, 59,* 12–16.

Vygotsky, L. S. (1978). *Mind in society: The development of higher psychological processes.* Cambridge, MA: Harvard University Press.

Wexler, L. J. (2020). "I would be a completely different teacher if I had been with a different mentor": Ways in which educative mentoring matters as novices learn to teach. *Professional Development in Education, 46*(2), 211–228.

Wood, D., Bruner, J. S., & Ross, G. (1976). The role of tutoring in problem solving. *Journal of Child Psychology and Psychiatry, 17,* 89–100.

CHAPTER SIX

Cultivating Clinical Coaching through Collaboration at Wright State University

Romena M. Garrett Holbert, Amy E. Elston, and Tracey A. Kramer

Clinical coaching requires teaching for P–12 student learning while simultaneously educating a teacher candidate within a unique social and political context. This chapter begins with an overview of guidelines and research from professional organizations that have shaped our approach to clinical educator selection and development, collaborations with schools and districts, and impacts on teacher candidates.

Next, we promote replicability by illuminating our structure and funding approach and how these enable our unit to be self-sustaining. Attention is paid to the specifics of our clinical model, including on-site professional development (PD), classroom follow-up, and larger conference-style offerings. After contextualizing our work, we discuss outcomes of our clinical program, including Candidate Preservice Assessment of Student Teaching (CPAST) and Education Teacher Performance Assessment (edTPA) data. The chapter concludes with reflections upon data, challenges, and opportunities for further development.

Research and Professional Organizations as Guiding Frameworks

The Office of Partnerships and Field Experiences (OPFE), the 2018 recipient of the Ohio Association of Teacher Educators (OATE) Outstanding Field Experience Program Award, works closely with the Teacher Education Department at Wright State University to deliver our clinical education program. Influenced by professional organizations such as ATE, NNER, and NAPDS, we find collaboration key to educator development (Association of Teacher Educators [ATE], 2016; National Association for Professional Development Schools [NAPDS], 2008; National Network for Educational Renewal [NNER], n.d.).

ATE Standards for Teacher Educators emphasize collaboration and PD to support clinical teacher educator capacity building (Holbert & Fisher, 2017). Our engagement with the NAPDS has influenced our structural design. Development of ongoing and reciprocal needs-based PD (essential 3); development of articulation agreements that delineate the roles and responsibilities of all involved (essential 6); building structures that allow all participants a forum for ongoing governance, reflection, and collaboration (essential 7); and engagement in work by college/university faculty and P–12 faculty in formal roles across institutional settings are hallmarks of our work drawn from NAPDS influences (NAPDS, 2008).

The authors' robust history in an NNER partner setting informs our choice of initiatives; we annually hold a network-based conference to foster simultaneous renewal of P–12 and higher education settings. In their ongoing practices, the authors demonstrate commitment to the four-part mission of the NNER: we acknowledge and respond to the shared responsibility for improving the realities of our schools, universities, and communities; believe that all students regardless of race, poverty, geography, or any other circumstance deserve equal access to high-quality learning and enriching life experiences; embody that students are to be both loved and challenged; and educate and prepare students to fully engage as considerate and critical citizens who know their value and capacity to make a profound impact in this world (NNER, 2019).

These beliefs prompt us to identify mentor teachers through a collaborative process in which district and building leadership and OPFE staff jointly invite teachers with both proven subject-area/grade-level expertise and demonstrated capacity for fostering professional growth to adopt the role of mentor teacher. Similarly, supervisors are identified through partnership connections; many are retired mentor teachers and partner district administrators.

Upon selection, the program assists clinical coaches (mentors and supervisors) in understanding teacher candidates' stages of concern (Fuller, 1969) and co-teaching/co-planning with them to support effective and contextualized teaching practice (Friend, 2008; Guise et al., 2017; Heck & Bacharach, 2016; Kinne et al., 2016; Kramer & Patel, 2010). Use of valid and reliable research-based measures enables us to assess hallmarks of quality teaching as represented in the Ohio Standards for the Teaching Profession in program outcomes (ODE, 2005; WSU-OPFE, 2018).

Program Structure

Scaffolded Internships

Three phases of field clinical practice, which include urban, rural, and suburban settings, are typical across our programs. Our clinical practice phases (figure 6.11) integrate research on stages of concern and hallmarks of quality teaching, to scaffold candidate and cooperating teacher development.

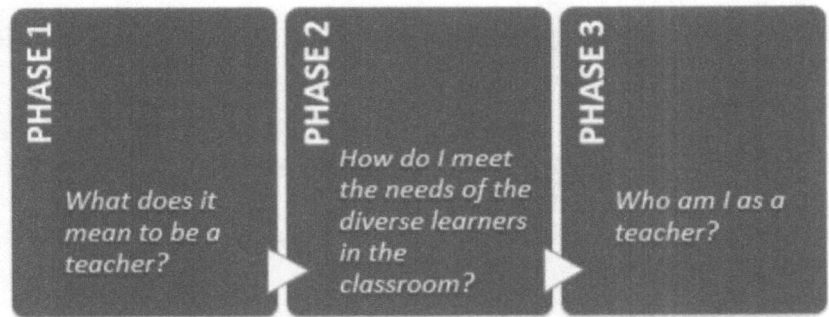

Figure 6.1. WSU Candidate Preparation Phases and Guiding Questions

Fuller advances three distinct phases of teacher concerns: self-related concerns, task-related concerns, and impact-related concerns (Fuller, 1969). The self-related concerns phase of early teaching reflects a focus on classroom management and evaluations. Next, teachers become concerned with lesson planning and grading papers, and, finally, teacher concerns shift to students and impacts of teaching on student success.

Professional development that aids educators' transition toward concerns about students is supported by identification and address of teacher concerns and provision of extensive support systems that involve peers, administrators, and their school districts (Bitan-Friedlander et al., 2004; Dass, 2001). The authors provide such PD to teacher candidates and partnering teacher educators. Each clinical experience builds upon prior practice, integrates the Ohio Standards for the Teaching Profession (OSTP), and supports transition across stages of concern in each OSTP-defined area of teaching practice:

1. Students
2. Content Knowledge
3. Assessment
4. Instruction
5. Learning Environment
6. Communication and Collaboration
7. Professional Development

Table 6.1 summarizes the order and key attributes of our placements.

Table 6.1. Clinical Practice Phase Scaffolding Including Teacher Candidate Experiences and Mentor Teacher Enactments

Clinical Practice Experiences (Early to Late)	Candidate Experience	Mentor Teacher Enactments
Phase I–Part I (One full or two half days weekly for 14 weeks) Assessed using a professional dispositions inventory	• Self-related concerns addressed • Organizational support roles with a focus on readiness for classroom presence • Typical activities include shadowing students, collecting behavioral data, teaching routine parts of modeled lessons	**Models/Provides:** schedule, key parts of the school day, academic and behavioral expectations of students **Initiates discussions about:** experience of entering profession/developing identity **Responds to:** Candidate initiative/independence, organizational and communication skills of candidate
Phase I–Part II (One full or two half days weekly for 14 weeks) Assessed using a professional dispositions inventory	• Self-related and task-related concerns integrated; focus placed on developing responsibility for typical elements of routine teaching • Enactment of routine tasks, scaffolded support to groups of students with similar learning needs • Typical activities include supporting students with makeup work, working with groups needing enrichment/remediation, assisting in design of assessments and/or rubrics	**Models/Provides:** examples/rationales for organization of session/day; examples of ways to learn about students' backgrounds/resources, sample lesson plans, questioning for candidate agency/critical thinking **Initiates discussions about:** classroom expectations, evidence of similarity or difference in student learning, relevance of student differences **Responds to:** Candidate evidence of initiative, respect for differences, punctuality, and ability to seek help when needed (among 23 dispositions)

Table 6.1.   (continued)

Clinical Practice Experiences (Early to Late)	Candidate Experience	Mentor Teacher Enactments
Phase II–same placement location will continue into phase III. In phase II, candidates begin with fall start of teacher school year and attend approximately 3 full days per week for 14 weeks. Assessed using PreCPAST	• Task-related concerns transition to focus on impact concerns as supported by methods course studies • Instructional support roles with a focus on co-teaching and enactment of teaching methods and strategies that promote educational quality for learner groups • Typical activities include creating individualized materials, adapting lessons for specific students, plan and execute transitions effectively, use technology for differentiation	**Models/Provides:** examples/rationales for lesson and/or assessment differentiation, discussion prompts, questioning for agency/critical thinking **Initiates discussions about:** evidence of similarity or difference in student learning, next steps based on classroom observations of groups of learners, rationales for instructional tools **Responds to:** Candidate recognition, interpretation, and articulation of data. Candidate communication skills, awareness of resources, and creativity
Phase III–a continuation of the same placement location from phase II, candidates attend all day every day concluding the week prior to the end of WSU's Spring Semester. Assessed using CPAST	• Impact concerns as primary focus, self/task as supports to impact • Classroom leadership roles with a focus on quality and equity for all learners • Typical activities include planning culturally relevant lessons, promoting critical thinking and idea integration, sequencing lessons, consistently promoting a safe and respectful classroom environment, designing varied assessments/using the data for planning	**Models/Provides:** examples/rationales for how multiple parts of lessons fit together, overarching aims addressed by the fit of instructional activities **Initiates discussions about:** professional learning opportunities, ways to engage families/communities in supporting student learning, ways to support students in using feedback **Responds to:** Candidate recognition, interpretation and articulation of data. Candidate communication skills, awareness of resources, and motivation toward professional growth

Professional Development Offerings

This program includes structures to intentionally support capacity building among our clinical coaches and university-based teacher educators and to link school- and university-based efforts. Opportunities are offered throughout the year for mentor teachers, teacher candidates, and university-based teacher educators to engage in PD that addresses topics relevant to them. Provision of PD serves multiple aims.

Teacher candidates gain opportunities to engage in PD alongside their mentor teacher, which supports relationship building and shared knowledge. Provision of free PD also brings together multiple groups of local educators, prompting networking across settings. Professional development offerings allow continued relationship building with our educational partners by celebrating outstanding instructional practices being implemented locally and recognizing the dynamic nature of education.

Particularly university-based teacher educators who are no longer in P–12 settings appreciate the opportunity to engage with current practitioners. Table 6.2 provides examples, descriptions, and typical participants for a range of OPFE offerings.

Table 6.2. Professional Development Offerings to Engage Those Connected to Clinical Experiences

Semester	Offering	Description	Potential Participants
Summer	Summer Partnership Institute	18–25 three- to six-hour sessions are offered on varied topics, such as English as a Second Language and Trauma-Informed Teaching	• Teacher candidates • Teachers • University-based teacher educators • P–12 administrators
Fall	Semester Professional Development	1.5 to 2 hours on a relevant topic, as expressed by partner school districts	• Teacher candidates • Teachers • University-based teacher educators • P–12 administrators
Fall	Clinical Practice Orientation	Takes place during finals week of the semester prior to the clinical practice to orient candidates to field expectations and offer strategies for success	• Teacher candidates • University-based teacher educators

Table 6.2. *(continued)*

Semester	Offering	Description	Potential Participants
Spring	WSUNER Learn Local Conference	Daylong series of sessions presented in March presented by local educators on topics independently suggested or requested by partners or OPFE	• Teacher candidates • Teachers • University-based teacher educators • P–12 administrators
Spring	Semester Professional Development	1.5 to 2 hours on a relevant topic, as expressed by partner school districts	• Teacher candidates • Teachers • University-based teacher educators • P–12 administrators
Spring	Clinical Practice Orientation	Takes place during finals week of the semester prior to the clinical practice to orient candidates to field expectations and offer strategies for success	• Teacher candidates • University-based teacher educators

Offering multiple PD opportunities, beginning in the summer prior to the start of internships, enables learning before and during the clinicals. For example, in response to teacher apprehensions regarding hosting candidates in a context of state mandates and pressures of high-stakes testing, a co-teaching session has been incorporated into the Summer Partnership Institute. This offering provides targeted preparation to mentor and candidate pairs to build relationships while alleviating concerns regarding teaching quality and maximizing the capacity for student learning through the active involvement of two educators. A session was also created to provide support and practice for mentor teachers regarding strategies for working with teacher candidates, such as offering constructive feedback to teacher candidates and developing a clearer understanding of the CPAST evaluation document.

Site-Based Supports

Each clinical internship includes on-site goal setting and support offered by a clinical coach. To begin, the supervisor, mentor teacher, and teacher candidate review expectations; contribute perspectives; and set goals, which can be measured through observation of classroom practice. A central role of the clinical coach is to be responsive to emergent strengths and needs. Regular engagement with mentor teachers along with skills practiced during OPFE training allows our supervisors to be able to provide resources and suggest approaches to conversations about progress and to serve as growth mindset–oriented facilitators of candidate and mentor teacher collaboration for student impact.

For particularly challenging cases, OPFE also provides a concern-conference process in which the director facilitates meetings on campus or on-site at the placement school to establish rigorous accountability checkpoints for candidates at risk of removal from placements. Our engagement with placement sites has also resulted in PD offerings that not only address mentor teacher concerns but also expand benefits to the entire faculty. Such offerings include trainings on co-teaching, cultural humility, and administration and analysis of newly developed state assessments.

Funding Approach

The OPFE, a distinct entity from departments served, receives its own budget from central administration and employs a self-sustaining approach to the funding of the clinical internship structure. Supervisor stipends are built into course fees paid by candidates and are calculated based on the phase of placement. In addition to this self-sustaining approach to supervision, expenses of mentor teacher honoraria and events are offset by making reduced-fee course credit available to those who elect credit hours in lieu of a certificate upon completion of PD, made possible by volunteer presenters organized by OPFE.

Data Analysis

CPAST and edTPA are primary assessments of candidate pedagogies and professional dispositions within our program. These data, coupled with assessments of additional programmatic priorities, inform program improvement.

CPAST

Data from the Candidate Preservice Assessment of Student Teaching (CPAST), a nationally normed assessment of student teaching ability, indicate that 99% of our 2017–2018 candidates met (46%) or exceeded (53%) CPAST expectations. Our candidates' pedagogy and dispositional assessment scores parallel state and national averages. Areas of particular strength include (b) Materials and Resources, (e) Learning Target and Directions, (g) Checking for understanding and adjusting instruction through formative assessment, and (i) Creating safe and respectful learning environments.

Our candidates exceed state and national averages with regard to (d) Implementing differentiated teaching methods and (m) Making connections to research and theory. Through clinical coaching, we have placed increased focus on areas for continued enhancement of our programs: (f) Critical thinking and (j) Data-guided instruction, both of which prove challenging across the nation.

The program faculty also assess professional dispositions using the last eight sections of the CPAST at the midpoint and culmination of the clinical internship. Areas in which our candidates surpass state and national averages include punctuality, meeting deadlines and obligations, and collaboration. The authors have noted that, though our candidates surpass state and national averages, limited opportunities to demonstrate effective communication with parents or legal guardians are available, so we are building scaffolded opportunities to draft conversation points for phone calls and conferences into our co-teaching approach.

Candidates score slightly below state and national averages on advocacy, so we have added this to conversation suggestions for mentor teachers. Trauma-informed teaching and differentiation to address concerns specific to students and communities are central parts of our PD; however, fluid integration into teaching practice does not tend to yield the explicit address necessary for documentation during formal observational assessments. Collaborative dialogue between clinical and campus-based teacher educators continues to explore whether to overtly call candidate attention to these areas with the aim of improving scores or to continue to allow integration in ways that emerge as a natural fit.

edTPA

The edTPA is a valid and reliable measure of candidate practice administered in the final term of student teaching. In Ohio, this assessment is not currently consequential to licensure and, as such, does not have a defined "cut" score to define passage rates. For example, if the cut scores were 35, 37, 39, or 42, 86%, 84%, 78%, or 69% of our 153 2017–2018 candidates (including those with incomplete submissions), respectively, would have been identified as passing.

Whereas some variation by content area is noted, analysis by task indicates that our candidate scores hover around a rating of three for each rubric.

Generally, we are satisfied with these scores, as our candidates also complete culminating research projects and student teach while composing their edTPA narratives. As an open enrollment institution, we find that many of our first-generation college students, particularly from rural areas, demonstrate significant strength in oral discourse and are still developing the writing style associated with the edTPA.

Areas we have built into mentor training to support transfer from oral to written communications include rubrics 9 Analyzing Subject-Specific Pedagogical Data (avg. 2.5), 10 Analyzing Teaching Effectiveness (avg. 2.6), and 13 Student Use of Feedback (avg. 2.6). Campus-based faculty partner to support this aim through written reflection assignments to facilitate candidate practice.

Teacher Candidate and Mentor Teacher Surveys

Surveys of mentor teachers are administered annually. In the 2017–2018 school-year survey, the 35 mentor teachers who responded to the online survey provided strong positive feedback about their experience with a teacher candidate and the resources and assistance they were provided throughout the semester. Ninety-four percent of the mentor teachers who responded agreed or strongly agreed that they were provided with clear expectations for mentor teacher roles; 97% indicated satisfaction with their candidate's contribution to the students and classroom; and 97% were satisfied with the assigned supervisor.

Mentor teachers were also asked to what degree they utilized their teacher candidates' supervisor throughout the semester. Sixty percent of the mentor teachers reported they use the supervisor to a large degree, while 37% responded "to a small degree." Though only 4% of our total pool of mentor teachers responded to the online survey, the data are consistent with informal communications provided by the vast majority of mentors.

Additionally, during the 2017–2018 period, 266 teacher candidates spanning all phases completed surveys that included questions based on a four-response Likert scale and also had an opportunity for open-ended responses. Overwhelmingly, the responses regarding OPFE, their supervisors, and their mentor teachers were on the positive end of the Likert scale; however, while considerably positive, some areas allowed for focused improvement.

The researchers continually work to streamline processes and instructions that come from OPFE in order to unify and clarify the message teacher candidates receive. In addition, when teacher candidates identify mentor teacher and supervisor strengths on the survey, feedback is commonly among the comments. Conversely, when teacher candidates provide comments emphasizing mentor teacher and supervisor weaknesses, a lack of substantive feedback is typically included in their statement. This feedback is shared on an annual basis with the supervisors.

Mentor teachers have a tremendous impact on teacher candidates' internship experiences. Forty-five percent of the responding teacher candidates provided positive feedback regarding their mentor teachers and how they helped them grow as an educator. Statements such as the following are echoed through many students' comments:

> Kari is an awesome CT (mentor teacher)! She was inviting and made me feel welcome in her classroom and the school. She was always willing to help me understand anything I had questions regarding anything in the education field. It was so nice to have a CT (mentor teacher) that is positive and encouraging. She was always willing to allow me to teach and be a part of the class.

Thirty percent of the responding teacher candidates left positive comments in regard to their experiences with their supervisors. Again, based on the teacher candidates' comments, constructive feedback is clearly valued. One student stated, "Anne was an amazing supervisor. She was organized at the beginning of the semester and had clear expectations set from the beginning. She was prompt in answering emails as well. She also gave great constructive feedback!"

Partnership Stakeholder Meeting

The CEHS utilizes an annual Partnership Stakeholder Meeting to invite teachers and administrators to the university to discuss the field-based internships and the processes that are currently in place to allow for updates and changes. Thirty-two teachers and administrators from partner districts attended the Spring 2019 meeting to provide input based on their experiences and suggestions for improvement. The meeting allowed participants to provide feedback about a teacher candidate formal lesson assessment feedback form that both mentor teachers and supervisors will utilize.

The teachers were asked to share their suggestions throughout the meeting if something came to mind, even if unrelated to the topic, that might be improved with a new perspective. Those teachers in attendance provided their insight into the teacher candidates' perspectives since many of those teachers have served as mentor teachers. The attendees suggested we work with faculty to lighten the load during phase 2, as many teacher candidates are coming into their clinical practice feeling overwhelmed by the amount of work. Also, they mentioned their appreciation for the monthly mentor teacher newsletter and how it might be helpful to share with the teacher candidates. The annual Partnership Stakeholder Meeting provides a unique opportunity to work with teachers and administrators to strengthen the clinical experience for teacher candidates.

Challenges and Opportunities

Implementation of our program has not been without challenges. However, our approach to addressing challenges is rooted in the same collaborative principles embodied in our approach to clinical teacher education and has served us well. The context of teacher education in Ohio has posed central challenges. We are not allowed to pay mentor teachers directly; we must pay the district, and whether/how teachers get paid depends on district policies.

We also exist in a context in which schools are positioned as competitors, which makes it difficult to leverage their resources in a unified way. These challenges prompt us to be flexible and creative about how to build and sustain relationships. Relationships are important not only to the candidates' experience of our program but also to maintaining accreditation by the Council for the Accreditation of Educator Preparation (CAEP) as an education preparation provider. District requests, state mandates, programs of study, and accreditation targets also evolve in ways that lead to change in the accountability demands on each of our partners. Clinical internships must be flexible to some degree to account for these changes and guidelines.

The beneficial opportunities associated with our P–12 partners not only far outweigh the challenges but also contribute to the improvement of our programs and instruction. We are committed to meeting the needs of all stakeholders as we articulated in our discussion of professional organization influences; collaboration not only helps us have a strong positive impact and meet stakeholder needs but also supports our ability to document accreditation responsibilities. One emergent opportunity was for us to reflect on our programmatic efforts through the lens of CAEP Standards (2015). For example, improvements to our program based on communication with stakeholders have included development of a lesson evaluation form better aligned to CPAST and more apt to encourage student growth (CAEP 2.3).

Mentor teachers also shared that more open-ended opportunities to write about candidate progress would be easier for them to complete. In addition, since the reporting of the data shared within this chapter, dialogue with mentor teachers has informed us of communication strategies that are helpful to engendering their continued engagement. Our mentor teacher newsletters (see https://traceykramer9.wixsite.com/wsuct/newsletters) are one example of particularly appreciated communication approaches. We have found our second year of the online newsletter to be an effective introduction of mentor teachers to online dialogue. During the 2018–2019 school year, we found increased mentor teacher survey responses as they have become more familiar with the process (CAEP 2.2).

Opportunities for improvement based on the collaborative address of challenges have also lent improvements to both teacher candidate and mentor teacher learning opportunities.

Additional feedback was provided to OPFE through open discussion and feedback from stakeholders. Mentor teachers often found candidates to be quite overwhelmed at the same points every semester.

Suggestions included providing an introduction to candidates prior to their arrival, streamlining our edTPA permission slip forms, and making sick days available to teacher candidates in their clinical internship (phase 3). Additional suggestions included that we lighten the coursework during phase 2 yearlong placements and provide additional supports to Adolescent to Young Adult (AYA) teacher candidates when working with middle-level students to support the integration of scaffolding into their lessons (CAEP 2.1).

Collaboration also led to the development of the Summer Partnership Institute session, held for the first time this summer for mentor teachers to improve their work with teacher candidates by learning to provide substantive feedback and clarity to the CPAST document (CAEP 2.2). Professional development offerings and opportunities are flexible as we discuss the needs mentor teachers and other partners share with us.

We do our best to accommodate those requests (CAEP 2.2). A past stakeholder request that we incorporated three years ago was to allow yearlong phase 2 and 3 candidates to be interviewed before mentor teachers commit to hosting them. This change has been met with appreciation by our partner districts. Additionally, the removal policy developed in 2016 was developed collaboratively with partners and faculty. In short, collaboration is at the heart of our program and has enabled us to experience success and sustain success across many forms of change.

References

Association of Teacher Educators (ATE). (2016). *Standards for clinical and field experiences.* https://ate1.org/field-experience-standards

Bitan-Friedlander, N., Dreyfus, A., & Milgrom, Z. (2004). Types of "teachers in training": The reactions of primary school science teachers when confronted with the task of implementing an innovation. *Teaching and Teacher Education, 20*(6), 607–619. doi.org/10.1016/j.tate.2004.06.007

Council for the Accreditation of Educator Preparation (CAEP). (2015). *Standard 2: Clinical partnerships and practice.* http://caepnet.org/standards/standard-2

Dass, P. M. (2001). Implementation of instructional innovations in K–8 science classes: Perspectives of inservice teachers. *International Journal of Science Education, 23*(9), 969–984. doi.org/10.1080/09500690010025021

Friend, M. (2008). Co-teaching: A simple solution that isn't simple after all. *Journal of Curriculum and Instruction*, 2(2), 9–19. doi.org/10.3776/joci.2008.v2n2p9-19

Fuller, F. F. (1969). Concerns of teachers: A developmental conceptualization. *American Educational Research Journal*, 6(2), 207–226. doi.org/10.3102/00028312006002207

Guise, M., Thiessen, K., Robbins, A., Habib, M., Stauch, N., & Hoellwarth, C. (2017). The evolution of clinical practice: Moving from traditional student teaching to co-teaching. In C. Martin & D. Polly (Eds.), *Handbook of research on teacher education and professional development* (pp. 1–33). Hershey, PA: IGI Global.

Heck, T. W., & Bacharach, N. (2016). A better model for student teaching. *Educational Leadership*, 73(4), 24–29.

Holbert, R. M. G., & Fisher, R. (2017). Classroom teachers as associated teacher educators: Applying ATE standards for teacher educators. In C. M. Crawford & S. L. Hardy (Eds.), *Redefining teacher preparation: Learning from experience in educator development* (pp. 1–22). Lanham, MD: Rowman & Littlefield.

Kinne, L. J., Ryan, C., & Faulkner, S. A. (2016). Perceptions of co-teaching in the clinical experience: How well is it working? *The New Educator*, 12(4), 343–360. doi.org/10.1080/1547688x.2016.1196802

Kramer, T., & Patel, N. (2010). *Co-teaching models and possible strategies*. https://docs.wixstatic.com/ugd/d6ccdf_ac8ba438a6dd48cf82e00f87e51fc3fc.pdf

National Association for Professional Development Schools (NAPDS). (2008). *9 essentials*. https://napds.org/nine-essentials/

National Network for Educational Renewal (NNER). (n.d.). *Four pillars and twenty postulates*. https://nnerpartnerships.org/about/four-pillars-twenty-postulates/

National Network for Educational Renewal. (2019). *NNER fast facts*. https://nnerpartnerships.org/nner-fast-facts/

Ohio Department of Education (ODE). (2005). *Ohio standards for the teaching profession*. Columbus, OH: ODE.

Wright State University College of Education and Human Services, Office of Partnerships and Field Experiences (WSU-OPFE). (2018, November). *Teacher candidate handbook: Candidate preservice assessment of student teaching* (CPAST). Internal document.

CHAPTER SEVEN

Using an Online Platform to Prepare Mentor Teachers as Clinical Coaches

Brooke K. Langan and Kathleen L. Post

Throughout the United States, more than 1,400 colleges and universities partner with thousands of school districts each year to afford mentoring to teacher candidates as part of a clinical internship experience (Childre & Van Rie, 2015; Greenbrook et al., 2011; Leshem, 2014).

While training high-quality mentors is an essential responsibility of education preparation programs (Paulson, 2014), the obstacles of time, travel, and readiness keep training numbers low, negatively impacting the effectiveness of mentor teachers (Caudle, 2013; Dinu, 2014; Leshem, 2014; Petrarca, 2013). While consistent, current, and meaningful training is cited as critical for all mentors (Childre & Van Rie, 2015; Leshem, 2014; Wood & Abdullah, 2016), there is a gap in the literature detailing how the use of the online platform can support the training of these boundary-spanning teacher educators.

Challenges and Opportunities

Quality mentor training can produce highly effective clinical coaches. When given relevant training to support the role, mentors become more comfortable and effective in supporting teacher candidates (Ambrosetti, 2014; Childre & Van Rie, 2015; Rakicioglu-Soylemez & Eroz-Tuga, 2014). Research indicates mentor teachers acknowledge there exists a lack of training opportunities specific enough to fulfill this role (Caudle, 2013; Childre & Van Rie, 2015; Leshem, 2014).

Educator preparation programs (EPP) must recognize this deficiency and make plans to provide robust training for mentor teachers that is easily accessible. Online delivery for training is one option emerging as a promising solution to address the obstacles of time, travel, and learner readiness (McDaniels et al., 2016; Petrarca, 2013).

With online training set within a mentor's contextual environment, the boundary-spanning teacher educator learns to develop as a supervisor in a personalized and active way. Training based in an andragogical framework and within the constructivist theory connects mentor teachers' lived experiences and supports opportunities to actively reflect and adapt learning. Additionally, the online learning environment provides opportunities to share, learn, and reflect with others in similar clinical settings. This collaborative, reflective process is essential to adult learning and forms a foundation for deep and meaningful acquisition of knowledge (Dorner & Kumar, 2016; Leshem, 2014; Liu & Li, 2012).

In an effort to address the problem of preparing mentor teachers while faced with the noted obstacles, an online training course was created to define role expectations, review university assessment protocols, and develop supervisory skills. The implementation of this training produced data detailing the impact the online platform had on the preparation of one university's mentor teachers. After three years implementing the online training course, mentor teachers expressed a clearer understanding of expectations and assessment procedures as well as acquired supervisory skills enhancing their mentoring of teacher candidates in the clinical setting.

As a result, the online training course not only illustrates an innovative way of supporting the development of mentor teachers as clinical coaches; it also offers an exemplar for other educator preparation programs searching for ways to promote ongoing, sustainable, just-in-time training for all mentors within the clinical setting.

Theoretical Framework

The dimensions of constructivism and andragogy support the development of an online training course for mentor teachers. Set within a contextual clinical environment, the mentor teacher learns to develop as a supervisor in a personalized and active way while the teacher candidate learns to develop as a teacher in a similar way, constructing meaning through experiences (Knowles, 1978). As adult learners, these school-based teacher educators require a different set of learning practices that should be incorporated into the development of training. Mentor teachers need opportunities to share, learn, and reflect with others in similar clinical coaching situations.

Online learning provides convenience and flexibility for adult learners without having to manipulate time and location to participate, allowing for personalization through self-organization and self-direction of learning (Sato & Haegele, 2018). Sato and Haegele (2018) articulated online opportunities empower the learner to personally acquire knowledge, recognize knowledge comes from a variety of sources, and provide individual responsibility for learning.

The personalized, experiential component is the connection between andragogy, constructivism, and online achievement for adults. Utilizing the online platform to support learning is reported to be an effective approach to adult learning (Caudle, 2013; Dinu, 2014; Leshem, 2014; Petrarca, 2013).

Literature Review

Making sure teacher candidates are equipped with an effective set of clinical experiences and a high-quality clinical coach during preservice education is fundamental. Mentored clinical experiences allow teacher candidates to apply what is learned, reflect on what is demonstrated, and revise accordingly (Childre & Van Rie, 2015; Dorner & Kumar, 2016). Mentored clinical practices are an essential component in enabling new teachers to blend content knowledge and pedagogy effectively. Ensuring strong mentor teachers are available to guide teacher candidates requires communication and long-term, research-driven training provided by the educator preparation program (Aspfors & Fransson, 2015; Lafferty, 2018; Russell & Russell, 2011).

Traditionally, training for mentor teachers has existed in one- to two-day, on-campus, face-to-face workshops consisting of reviewing the program's clinical internship manual, a general overview of the roles and responsibilities of the mentor teacher, and contact with university officials (Ambrosetti, 2014; Lafferty, 2018). As Childre and Van Rie (2015) and Petrarca (2013) contended, without a travel requirement, having 24-hour, self-paced access, online delivery of training for mentor teachers has great potential.

Teaching is an isolated profession where teachers are often instructing in classrooms for hours per day without making practical connections with others in the field. Having the ability to network with other professionals allows teachers to learn from one another via a learning community (Kelly et al., 2018). The online platform seems to be an appropriate choice for networked learning of teachers.

While training is cited as critical for all mentor teachers (Childre & Van Rie, 2015; Leshem, 2014; Wood & Abdullah, 2016), there is a gap in the literature detailing how the exclusive use of an online training course can support the mandated training requirements. Through the process of implementing an online training program, the following questions were addressed. What are mentor teachers' perceptions of learning in an online environment? What impact does an online training program have on a mentor teacher's understanding of their roles and responsibilities, comfort level as a supervisor, and ability to accurately assess based on a shared unit-wide assessment approach?

Program Background and Research Method

Faced with many of the same training obstacles as educator preparation programs across the country, one midsized public university in the northeastern region of the United States chose to implement an online approach to training its mentor teachers. With over 20 partner districts serving over 150 teacher candidates per year, it was imperative for the university to develop an approach to revise the training for its 300+ mentors each year. With time and geographic access limited, the online platform was deemed a plausible solution.

Methodology

While the initial online training module for mentor teachers has been implemented since Spring 2017, iterations of the module have been developed as the training needs of the mentors were identified. Annual data collected from course surveys were analyzed to explore how the online training course impacted mentors' understandings of roles and responsibilities, specifically role expectations, common assessment scoring, and supervisory skills.

Training platform. Finding a common and accessible platform for training posed the first obstacle for the identified educator preparation program. Many universities and school districts subscribe to varied learning management systems (LMSs), which do not interact with one another. These campus-specific systems leave field experience offices unable to provide access to the off-campus mentor teachers. Due to the geographically varied participant population needing access to the online training module, the use of the free version of the online LMS, Canvas, was chosen as the best tool for granting access to all mentor teachers.

The evolution of training. The field experience office created a free account within Canvas and built the initial training module in Spring 2017, based upon the needs at that time. As a new field experience director began the position in Fall 2016, it was determined a set of standard mentor teacher expectations needed to be defined in Spring 2017 for the first iteration of the training course. With this goal identified, the traditional clinical practice mentor teacher handbook was transferred from print to a digital introductory component of the online training module.

The introductory module centered on a variety of components related to mentor teacher expectations. The module began with an introduction of purpose from the field experience director. Next, the course guided the participants to introduce themselves to other participating mentors on a discussion board, sharing district, grade level, years of teaching experience, and mentoring experiences. After this informal discussion, the course delved into general expectations, including informal and formal observation guidelines. In addition, all due dates were presented in the form of a printable checklist.

Additional content regarding the university's data management program, Tk20, included video tutorials on completing the required university observation forms, payment card, and supporting documentation. To monitor participation, an ungraded quiz was embedded to check for basic understanding of Tk20. After the review of assessment requirements, mentor teachers were given information about the university's expectations for student teacher professionalism (attire, appearance, demeanor), attendance, lesson planning, and on-campus practica.

The final section of the introductory module asked the mentors to participate in another discussion forum where they shared personal clinical internship expectations, which may differ from the previously shared university expectations. This collaborative approach to defining expectations was to make sure the university was aware and addressing these expectations in education preparation courses as well as in clinical internship practicum sessions.

Online survey. At the conclusion of the introductory training module, participants were asked to complete an online survey focused on the purpose and goals of the module. During its first implementation, the online training module survey centered on three main objectives: a better understanding of university expectations for mentor teachers, structured support for the use of the university's data management system (Tk20), and common ground between university and mentor teacher expectations for teacher candidates.

During the first iteration of the online training module, 124 mentor teachers completed the end-of-module survey (see table 7.1). Surveyed on a 5-point Likert scale, with 1 representing strongly disagree and 5 representing strongly agree, most mentor teachers agreed the three module focus areas supported them, with the averaged response well above the midrange on the 5-point Likert scale.

Table 7.1. Response Means for Online Mentor Teacher Training Module—Spring 2017

	M	SD
This module gave me a better understanding of what is expected of me as a mentor teacher for ESU.	4.33	0.72
The resources provided me with a better understanding of how to operate Tk20.	4.23	0.80
I feel that my expectations for teacher candidates is similar to ESU expectations for teacher candidates.	4.67	0.51

Note: $n = 124$; 5-point Likert scale

Year 2: Introducing unit-wide assessments. Motivated by preliminary positive results, the online training course evolved for a new purpose by the university's Teacher Education Unit (TEU) during the 2017–2018 academic year. The TEU, in preparation for national accreditation through the Council for the Accreditation of Educator Preparation (CAEP), developed and approved common unit-wide assessments for all clinical experience semesters. With a new assessment strategy impacting over 600 boundary-spanning teacher educators, mentors, university faculty members, clinical internship supervisors, and teacher candidates, it was decided to utilize the online platform to introduce the new assessments and to provide instruction to ensure standardized scoring for all.

For the mentor teachers of the 2017–2018 academic year, this meant the addition of another module to the previously designed training course. A module on unit-wide assessments (UWA) was developed to include an explanatory introduction by the dean of the College of Education as well as an introduction to each of the four assessments. The newly designed module included a video review of each assessment rubric; interactive, video-based scenarios with nongraded quizzing to aid in reliable scoring practices; and feedback on predetermined anchor scores for each of the exemplars.

While the design of the unit-wide assessment training lingered into the Fall 2017 semester, data on its implementation was not available until the Spring 2018 semester (see table 7.2). The survey included a new question for mentors to rate the unit-wide assessment module and resources. While the average results for the training in each semester remained well above the midrange of the 5-point Likert scale, there was a noticeable decline in participation between the fall and spring semesters.

The authors attribute this decline to the rigor and time requirements needed to complete the unit-wide assessments module of the training. The introductory expectations module averaged three hours to complete, while the unit-wide assessment module averaged more than five hours for completion.

Table 7.2. Response Means for Online Mentor Teacher Training Module—Fall 2017 and Spring 2018

	Fall 2017 n = 39		Spring 2018 n = 36	
	M	SD	M	SD
This module of the training gave me a better understanding of what is expected of me as a mentor teacher for ESU.	4.18	0.87	4.14	0.54
The resources provided me with a better understanding of how to operate Tk20.	4.16	0.87	4.11	0.61
I feel that my expectations for teacher candidates is similar to ESU expectations for teacher candidates.	N/A	N/A	4.14	0.75
The resources on unit-wide assessment scoring are beneficial to me as a mentor teacher.	4.58	0.79	4.27	0.61

Note: 5-point Likert scale

Year 3: Focusing on the supervisory needs of cooperating teachers. The third and most recent year of online training was developed based on the supervisory needs of mentor teachers. With unit-wide assessment training complete for the majority of teachers who mentor, the surveys from the previous course iterations suggested mentors wanted to learn more about supporting the needs of another adult and providing beneficial feedback. Additionally, mentors requested more structured weekly reminders on course topics. Based on this feedback, the online training was expanded to include a module on supervisory tips supported by weekly overview emails.

The supervisory module for mentor teachers included a weekly focus on the following topics: Week One—Co-Teaching & Metacognition; Week Two—Planning & Classroom Management; Week Three—Building the Supervisory Relationship; Week Four—Providing Constructive Feedback; Week Five—Focusing on Affective Education; and Week Six—Recommending the Teacher Candidate.

The newly redesigned course was unveiled in Spring 2019. With previous completion of the introductory expectations module and unit-wide assessments module, mentor teachers were asked to initially review the expectations and UWA modules before interacting with the supervisory module weekly to learn more about the topics shared in the weekly email overviews.

The weekly email announcement served as a reminder for mentors to focus on the week's topic and to explore the published online resources for themselves and with their teacher candidate.

For the third iteration of the course, the assessment of the course was modified to a pre- and postassessment to identify gains after course completion. One hundred twenty-eight mentor teachers completed a preassessment and postassessment (see table 7.3). Questions were rated on a 4-point Likert scale and showed gains in the average response from the preassessment to the postassessment.

Table 7.3. Response Means for Online Mentor Teacher Training Module—Spring 2019

	Preassessment		Postassessment	
	M	SD	M	SD
Please rate your understanding of the roles and responsibilities of an ESU mentor teacher after completing this online course.	3.24	0.54	3.49	0.51
How comfortable are you now as a supervisor for another adult (teacher candidate) after completing this course?	3.65	0.52	3.83	0.38

Note: n = 128; 4-point Likert scale

Additionally, question 5 asked mentor teachers to describe their preferred delivery of training (see figure 7.1). In the postassessment, email resources, self-guided training, and the online course were perceived more positively over in-person at school/district group instructor–led workshops, leading the authors to believe the online course and weekly emails were beneficial for providing training to mentor teachers.

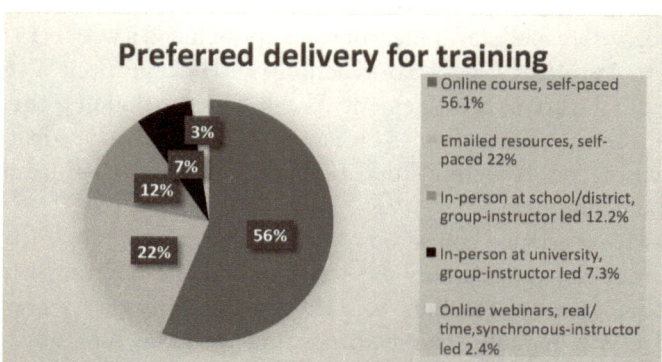

Figure 7.1. Mentor teachers preferred delivery mode for training

Findings, Outcomes, and Learning

In this study, the impact of the online platform for training mentor teachers was examined over a three-year period to understand how an online training course for mentors impacted the understanding of roles and responsibilities, specifically role expectations, common assessment scoring, and supervisory skills.

The survey data indicated mentors appreciated having all training resources in one readily accessible location, enabling them to better understand role expectations and responsibilities. In addition, mentors noted similar teacher candidate expectations with the university when provided with the university expectations. Finally, in the most recent iteration of the online course, mentors strongly indicated their preference for online, self-paced, digital support, rather than synchronous online or in-person instructor-led training.

These results indicate the online platform as a viable and preferred option for training mentor teachers as clinical coaches. The online training modules diminished the barriers of time and geography, which often serve as obstacles for education preparation programs in training mentors. While the results of this study support the online platform, it should be noted the authors acknowledge that no single training method is completely effective for training all mentors. Moreover, while the majority of mentors in this study preferred online delivery of training, there still exists a minority who prefer in-person and synchronous learning. These findings support the need for a differentiated training model by education preparation programs that examine the personal learning needs of all who serve as clinical coaches.

Research-Based Implications

The results of this data review can guide higher education preparation programs with the knowledge of how an online training course may be one method that enables mentors to better understand their roles and responsibilities (Childre & Van Rie, 2015; Petrarca, 2013). Additionally, the data brings to light the need for differentiated models of training within education preparation programs (Ferreira et al., 2018; Qian et al., 2018).

Further research is necessary to better understand the technology tools available and the varied modes of learning for mentor teachers. Continued research should also focus on the expansion of the learning needs of mentors within the clinical setting (Ferreira et al., 2018; Sato & Haegele, 2018). While the development of an online training course illustrates an innovative way of supporting the development of mentor teachers as clinical coaches, it also offers an exemplar for other education preparation programs searching for ways to promote ongoing, sustainable, just-in-time training for all mentoring teachers.

References

Ambrosetti, A. (2014). Are you ready to be a mentor? Preparing teachers for mentoring pre-service teachers. *Australian Journal of Teacher Education, 39*(6), 30–42. doi.org/10.14221/ajte.2014v39n6.2

Aspfors, J., & Fransson, G. (2015). Research on mentor education for cooperating teachers of newly qualified teachers: A qualitative meta-synthesis. *Teaching and Teacher Education, 48,* 75–86.

Caudle, L. A. (2013). Using a sociocultural perspective to establish teaching and social presences within a hybrid community of mentor teachers. *Adult Learning, 24*(3), 112–120.

Childre, A., & Van Rie, L. (2015). Mentor teacher training: A hybrid model to promote partnering in candidate development. *Rural Special Education Quarterly, 34*(1), 10–16.

Dinu, M. (2014). Online professional development: A platform for creativity and innovation in teacher's training. *Elearning and Software for Education, 2,* 137–141. doi:10.12753/2066-026X-14-074\

Dorner, H., & Kumar, S. (2016). Online collaborative mentoring for technology integration in pre-service teacher education. *TechTrends, 60*(1), 48–55. doi:10.1007/s11528-015-0016-1

Ferreira, D., MacLean, G., & Center, G. E. (2018). Andragogy in the 21st century: Applying the assumptions of adult learning online. *ICU Language Research Bulletin, 32,* 10–19.

Greenbrook, J., Pomerance, L., & Walsh, K. (2011). Student teaching in the United States. National Council on Teacher Quarterly. www.nctq.org/dmsView/Student_Teaching_United_States_NCTQ_Report

Kelly, N., Russell, N., Kickbusch, S., Barros, A., Dawes, L., & Rasmussen, R. (2018). Online communities of teachers to support situational knowledge: A design-based study. *Australasian Journal of Educational Technology, 34*(5), 150–166.

Knowles, M. S. (1978). Andragogy: Adult learning theory in perspective. *Community College Review, 5*(3), 9–20.

Lafferty, K. K. (2018). The difference explicit preparation makes in cooperating teacher practice. *Teacher Education Quarterly, 45*(3), 73–95.

Leshem, S. (2014). How do teacher cooperating teachers perceive role, does it matter? *Asia-Pacific Journal of Teacher Education, 42*(3), 261–274.

Liu, L., & Li, W. (2012). Using an online learning management system as collaborative media to support adult learning: Needs assessment. *International Journal of Technology in Teaching and Learning*, 8(2), 135–145.

McDaniels, M., Pfund, C., & Barnicle, K. (2016). Creating dynamic learning communities in synchronous online courses: One approach from the center for the integration of research, teaching and learning (CIRTL). *Online Learning*, 20(1), 110–129.

Paulson, D. M. (2014). Perceptions of cooperating teachers concerning the student teaching field experience (Doctoral dissertation).

Petrarca, D. (2013). A promising practicum pilot-exploring associate teachers' access and interactions with a web-based learning tool. *Interdisciplinary Journal of E-Learning and Learning Objects*, 9(2013), 149–170.

Qian, Y., Hambrusch, S., Yadav, A., & Gretter, S. (2018). Who needs what: Recommendations for designing effective online professional development for computer science teachers. *Journal of Research on Technology in Education*, 50(2), 164–181.

Rakicioglu-Soylemez, A., & Eroz-Tuga, B. (2014). Mentoring expectations and experiences of prospective and cooperating teachers during practice teaching. *Australian Journal of Teacher Education (Online)*, 39(10), 146–168.

Russell, M. L., & Russell, J. A. (2011). Mentoring relationships: Cooperating teachers' perspectives on mentoring student interns. *Professional Educator*, 35(1), 16–35.

Sato, T., & Haegele, J. A. (2018). Physical teachers' engagement in online adapted physical education graduate professional development. *Professional Development in Education*, 44(2), 272–286.

Wood, N. E., & Abdullah, A. (2016). Two approaches for increasing student learning and professional development. *Journal of Nonprofit Education and Leadership*, 6(4), 316–330.

CHAPTER EIGHT

Practice-Based Coaching to Impact Early Childhood Teacher Candidate Uptake of Evidence-Based Practice in Clinical Internship

Toni Miguel

Early childhood programs across the United States have proliferated due to compelling research demonstrating the long-term benefits on young children's school readiness and future academic and social success (Barnett et al., 2017). As a result, there is an increasing need for highly qualified teachers to staff early childhood programs, especially teachers who are trained in using evidence-based teaching practices to ensure advantageous learning and development outcomes for children (IOM & NRC, 2015).

But many novice teachers enter the field with underdeveloped teaching practices and associated negative feelings of self-efficacy in their teaching (Reineke et al., 2011). Despite the existence of highly effective, evidence-based classroom teaching strategies, there is a significant gap between what is known about early childhood teaching and the teaching practices of novice early childhood educators.

A particular area of interest in the education of young children is social, emotional, and behavioral development. In fact, children entering kindergarten with higher levels of social–emotional competence are more successful in both the academic and social aspects of school (La Paro & Pianta, 2000). However, research has shown upward of 10% to 20% of children in early childhood programs exhibit low levels of social–emotional competence, often resulting in challenging behaviors (e.g., hitting, kicking, spitting, and throwing objects) (Brauner & Stephens, 2006).

Unresolved, persistent challenging behaviors can lead to harsh disciplinary practices, including suspension and expulsion from educational and childcare settings. Teachers feel unprepared to support the social–emotional development of children, especially those who demonstrate more intensive social–emotional needs (e.g., challenging behavior), which puts children at risk for poor outcomes (Reineke et al., 2011).

The early childhood landscape is fractured and varied with children between the ages of zero and five being served in a wide array of educational settings (Hustedt & Barnett, 2011). Similarly, preservice early childhood teacher education is fragmented. The preparation of early childhood educators varies dramatically from K–12 teacher education. Teacher candidates at the K–12 level are educated in education departments and have similar certification requirements. Early childhood teacher candidates may be educated in one of several disciplines (e.g., family studies, human development, and child development) and have varying requirements based on setting, programs, and ages of children served.

Some early childhood educators never attend formal university-based teacher education (Ryan & Gibson, 2016). Traditionally, early childhood teacher education strengths have been in attending to views of the whole child development and learning (Couse & Recchia, 2016). However, very little research has been done to understand the impact of early childhood teacher education programs on teacher practice and child learning (Ryan & Gibson, 2016). Even less is known about early childhood teacher education impact to teacher candidates use of evidence-based practices to support social–emotional competence.

There is a clear need for effective teacher education to prepare early childhood teachers to facilitate the social–emotional competence of young children. Fortunately, there has been ample research conducted with practicing teachers to support young children's social and emotional competence (Hemmeter et al., 2015; Snyder et al., 2015). These studies indicate children in classes with teachers who successfully implement evidence-based practices have lower rates of challenging behavior and better social–emotional competence overall. Leaders have called for additional scholarship and intervention in the field of early childhood teacher education given the fragmentation of systems across early care and education services (IOM & NRC, 2015).

Researchers are now using coaching as a way to successfully impact teachers' practice, specifically their use of evidence-based practices (Rock et al., 2014). Coaching can be defined as "an ongoing, dynamic, and interactive process wherein an expert practitioner models, supports, and encourages an adult to reflect on and subsequently improve one's practice" (Gupta &

Daniels, 2012, p. 206). Coaching has been empirically linked to changes in teacher behavior and sustained use of practices (Gupta & Daniels, 2012).

However, little is known about the applicability of coaching professional development models in university-based early childhood teacher education. If there is an absence of practice-focused teacher education strategies, this may contribute to the difficulties novice early childhood teachers face in making meaningful change in their practice prior to entering the field.

In this chapter, the theory driving clinical coaching methods and research supporting clinical coaching will be explored through the lens of university-based teacher preparation programs and early childhood settings in particular. An emerging model of clinical coaching, practice-based coaching (PBC), will be considered as a method for university-based teacher educators and mentor teachers to use with teacher candidates during the clinical internship (NCQTL, 2020). Recent research demonstrating the efficacy of PBC with teacher candidates to impact their use of evidence-based practices and feelings of teaching self-efficacy will be presented.

Literature and Theory

Similar to the movement in professional development toward the uptake of evidence-based practices, university-based teacher education programs are considering high-leverage practices that place teacher practice at the center of professional preparation (Ball & Forzani, 2009). Recent calls for shifts to a focus on teacher practice have aimed at increasing the relevancy of university-based teacher education programs (Blue Ribbon Panel, 2010).

In early childhood, specifically, there is a critical need for teachers who understand and are able to do the incredibly important and nuanced work of educating and caring for young children. Early childhood educators are tasked with supporting children in the most critical years of neural activity along with attending to the complex needs associated with increased racial, cultural, and linguistic diversity among children aged zero to five (IOM & NRC, 2015).

There is a limited research base in the field of early childhood teacher education examining high-leverage teacher education methods impacting teacher candidate practice. Horm et al. (2013) attempted to illustrate this fact by synthesizing research in early childhood teacher education literature. The researchers found significant gaps and made recommendations for the kind of research most needed to impact early childhood teacher education. The authors call for research integrating information across boundaries of clinical practice and professional development to inform the field more broadly. Coaching is a promising teacher education practice to be used in early childhood university-based teacher education.

Theoretical Foundations of Coaching

Coaching draws on multiple theoretical models or frameworks to explain the relationship between coaching interactions and teacher practice. First, coaching uses adult learning principles as described by Knowles (1970). Coaching models allow learning and application to occur nearly simultaneously, as it is situated in a practice-centered arena (clinical internship). Coaching also embraces the theory of teacher change (Guskey, 1982) due to its direct focus on teacher practice as a way to indirectly change teacher attitudes and beliefs.

Lastly, a teacher's sense of self-efficacy (Bandura, 1997) can be more easily supported through a coaching model of teacher education as the coach and teacher candidate enter into a responsive relationship where the coach actively attends to the teacher candidate's needs to promote his or her learning and development of teaching practices. For teacher candidates and novice teachers, research has shown increased self-efficacy regarding teaching practices results in better outcomes for children (Caprara et al., 2006).

Research Foundations of Coaching in Early Childhood

In professional development research, there are two relevant reviews of the early childhood coaching literature finding similar results. First, Gupta and Daniels (2012) found coaching is typically used to complement other in-service professional development (i.e., workshops or coursework) and the combination proved to make positive impacts on teacher practice and child outcomes. Second, Artman-Meeker et al. (2015) focused on the specific strategies and features of coaching. In both reviews, the authors found most of the literature did not describe coaching interventions in sufficient detail to glean details regarding duration, frequency, intensity, or dosage of coaching interventions.

The use of coaching in early childhood university-based teacher education literature is only recently emerging. Barton and colleagues (2013) used a coaching intervention with early childhood teacher candidates to increase their use of teaching practices to support play with young children with disabilities. The study showed that training alone made no difference in teacher candidate use of the targeted teaching practices but coaching made an immediate and lasting impact. An additional study looked at the use of coaching delivered via email for teacher candidates with promising results (Barton et al., 2016). The next section will illustrate, in more detail, the use of a specific coaching model for early childhood teacher candidates.

Practice-Based Coaching

Practice-based coaching (PBC) is a framework for coaching early childhood educators developed through partnerships from multiple researchers and stakeholders, including implementation science and Head Start's professional development resources. PBC is defined as "a cyclical process for supporting preschool practitioners' use of effective teaching practices that leads to positive outcomes for children" (Snyder et al., 2015, p. 134).

The practices referred to here are the specific teacher actions or behaviors that manipulate the physical, temporal, or social environment to support advantageous child outcomes. This differs from other coaching models because it has an explicit focus on supporting practices considered evidence based and high leverage, rather than relationship-based coaching practices that are nondirective and context driven (e.g, Rush & Shelden, 2011).

The framework for PBC holds effective teaching practices, or evidence-based teaching practices, at the core. The teaching practices chosen may be different for a given teacher candidate but should always stem from evidence-based or recommended practices for a particular teaching field. PBC uses an ongoing cycle of shared goals and action planning, focused observation, and reflection and feedback (see additional details on PBC implementation below). PBC does not aim to directly impact the internal drivers that contribute to teaching practice (i.e., dispositions, attitudes, and feelings of self-efficacy). However, it is important to note that teachers who engage in PBC may have indirect changes to these internal drivers of teaching practice.

Research Supporting the Use of PBC

Research with practicing teachers has shown PBC to be highly effective in stimulating teacher change. In one study, coaches in an early childhood classroom used PBC to train teachers in Behavioral, Emotional, and Social Training: Competent Learners Achieving School Success (BEST in CLASS), an intervention model to increase social–emotional competence and decrease challenging behaviors of preschool children. Using an experimental design, researchers were able to demonstrate teachers in the PBC condition significantly increased their use of the BEST in CLASS practices and maintained these differences postintervention (Sutherland et al., 2015).

Given the importance of shifting toward a focus on teacher preparation methods that highlight teaching practice, it is important to examine the implementation of PBC in university-based teacher education programs. The PBC cycle and tools used in a university-based teacher education program are described below.

PBC cycle and tools. There are three distinct phases of a PBC cycle that occur within the context of a collaborative partnership. First, the collaborative partnership refers to the interactions between the teacher candidate and the teacher educator to provide space for reflection, asking questions, and gathering information. A collaborative partnership can be established through relationship-building strategies (i.e., rapport, shared understandings, and mutual expectations) over the course of a teacher education program. Then, in the clinical internship, the teacher educator and teacher candidate are prepared to engage in PBC.

Shared goals and action planning. In the shared goals and action planning phase of PBC, the teacher educator, in collaboration with the teacher candidate, assesses the teacher candidate's needs, sets goals for coaching, and creates a working action plan. The needs assessment must delineate specific, observable teaching practices that are evidence based and high leverage for the particular setting (i.e., early childhood vs. elementary or general education vs. special education).

The needs assessment instrumentation can be varied; however, it is important to capture both quantitative and qualitative data on the teacher candidate's use of practices (see an example of a tool in the next section). For example, the teacher educator may observe using a tool to measure the number of times the teacher candidate uses open-ended questions while reading aloud while also qualitatively noting the actual questions. An example of a needs assessment would list five to seven specific, observable teaching practices followed by columns to record data. For each teaching practice, there is a space to denote quantitative data (i.e., frequency counts or interval recording) and qualitative data (i.e., anecdotal notes on the teacher candidate's use of teaching practices).

The data from the needs assessment is shared with the teacher candidate. Goals are set in a shared process, balancing the knowledge of the teacher educator and the priorities of the teacher candidate. For example, the teacher educator might target literacy practices for reading aloud, and the teacher candidate then chooses to focus on asking more open-ended questions.

Focused observation. In the next phase, the teacher educator engages in focused observations similar to usual clinical coaching practices. In the PBC cycle, focused observations are guided by the shared goals and working action plan. The teacher educator may use a tool to capture varied data on the teacher candidate's use of selected practices. An example of a focused observation tool is shared in table 8.1.

Table 8.1. Example of a Focused Observation Tool

	Teaching Practices								
Interval	Teacher offers general guidance to children to select activities or use materials to promote engagement.		Teacher communicates with children on eye level.		Teacher assists individual children in selecting center activities and becoming actively engaged.		Teacher comments positively on children who are engaged in activities.		Qualitative Notes
1	1	0	1	0	1	0	1	0	
2	1	0	1	0	1	0	1	0	
3	1	0	1	0	1	0	1	0	
4	1	0	1	0	1	0	1	0	

Note: 1= Observed; 0 = Not observed; add rows as needed for length of observation.

In the top row, the selected teaching practices are noted. The observation is broken into one-minute intervals, and the teacher educator can mark whether the teaching practice is observed. There is also space to make qualitative notes on the teacher's use of practices. This tool can also be translated into a Qualtrics app, where the teacher educator can collect data and electronically store and share the data with the teacher candidate.

The focused observation of the teacher educator does not stray outside of the shared goals and action plan. This is why it is critical to select high-leverage practice areas at the outset of the PBC cycle. For example, in early childhood teacher education, social–emotional competence is considered a high-leverage content area. So an early childhood teacher educator may observe teacher candidates on their use of specific practices to support social–emotional competence only, rather than the entire spectrum of effective early childhood teacher practice.

Reflection and feedback. The third phase of the PBC cycle occurs in the context of a debriefing meeting between the teacher educator and teacher candidate. Here, mutual consideration is given to the results of the focused observation to identify successes, challenges, and areas for future improvement. Feedback is shared by both the teacher educator and teacher candidate to help achieve the goals set after the initial needs assessment. In this debriefing meeting, a working action plan is revised given the results of focused observation and the reflection and feedback of the teacher candidate and teacher educator. For example, it may be decided that the goal was achieved and it is time to return to the original needs assessment to identify other teaching practices for focus. Or additional strategies and resources may be identified to further support the teacher candidate's goal. Table 8.2 shows an example of a working action plan.

Table 8.2. Example of a Teaching Practices Working Action Plan

	Date 1	Date 2	Date 3
Teaching practice that I will focus on My goal for this practice What strategies will I use to help me achieve this goal? How will I know I've achieved this goal? What supports and/or resources do I need?			
Future coaching dates:			

Note: Add columns to the right for each coaching session.

Sample teaching practices, goals, assessment procedures, and strategies/resources are denoted in the left column. The coach and the teacher candidate mutually agree on a teaching practice to develop goals, assessment procedures, and strategies for implementation. Then, a specific, observable goal related to the teaching practice(s) can be developed along with how the goal will be assessed and any specific resources and supports the teacher candidate needs to achieve the goal. Each time the teacher educator and teacher candidate meet to engage in reflection and feedback, the working action plan will add another column where focus practice areas, goals, assessment, and resources/strategies are revised. As the working action plan expands for each coaching session, the teacher candidate and teacher educator have a visual reminder of all the teaching practices the teacher candidate has mastered within clinical coaching.

PBC Research in Clinical Internship Settings

In the study described below, the researcher used a multiple-baseline single-case design to study the impact of PBC on teacher candidates' use of evidence-based practices to support young children's social–emotional competence. Additional data on teacher candidates' sense of self-efficacy related to the use of these practices was collected.

Three teacher candidates were recruited from university-based early childhood teacher education programs to engage in PBC with the research team during their clinical internship semester. PBC was introduced to each teacher candidate at different time points to demonstrate experimental control for a single-case study design (Kazdin, 2011). Visual inspection of the data demonstrated a clear functional relationship between the implementation of PBC and teacher candidates' use of targeted practices. A predictable baseline pattern for each participant was established where use of evidence-based practices to support social–emotional competence was in the range of 42% to 57% (average 48%). After the introduction of PBC, the participants' average use of practices increased to 77% use of evidence-based practices (range 76% to 77%). This constituted a 60% increase in teacher candidates' use of targeted, evidence-based teaching practices from baseline to intervention for supporting the social–emotional competence of young children. Participants were able to maintain their use of evidence-based practices in their clinical settings after the cessation of coaching (average 70%; range 63% to 84%).

Survey data using the Teachers' Sense of Self-Efficacy Scale (Tschannen-Moran & Hoy, 2001) was compared prestudy and post-PBC. Two-tailed t-tests found a statistically significant positive difference between feelings of teaching self-efficacy prestudy and post-PBC, $t(14) = 8.10$, $p < .01$. Given the low n of the study ($n = 3$), it is difficult to generalize these findings, but it provides a promising direction for the use of PBC in clinical internship experiences to make significant changes to teacher candidates' feelings of self-efficacy. Social validity survey results demonstrated favorable or very favorable results for all components of the PBC intervention. One participant stated, "I really enjoyed this study and feel I've had a shift of perspective because of this opportunity."

Conclusion

Given the ample research demonstrating coaching can positively impact practicing teachers and make significant contributions to positive child outcomes, it is important to consider ways these can translate to preservice settings. Recent research shows promising results for the efficacy of using PBC with teacher candidates. This poses important implications for the structure of clinical practice in university-based teacher education programs to engage in PBC-style observations with targeted feedback and reflection. Shifting clinical internship practices toward a greater explicit focus on targeted, high-leverage, evidence-based teaching practices will impact both teacher and child outcomes.

References

Artman-Meeker, K., Fettig, A., Barton, E. E., Penney, A., & Zeng, S. (2015). Applying an evidence-based framework to the early childhood coaching literature. *Topics in Early Childhood Special Education, 35*(3), 183–196.

Ball, D., & Forzani, F. M. (2009). The work of teaching and the challenge for teacher education. *Journal of Teacher Education, 60*(5), 497–511.

Bandura, A. (1997). Self-efficacy: Toward a unifying theory of behavioral change. *Psychological Review, 84*(2), 191–215.

Barnett, W. S., Friedman-Krauss, A. H., Weisenfeld, G. G., Horowitz, M., Kasmin, R., & Squires, J. H. (2017). *The state of preschool 2016: State preschool yearbook*. National Institute for Early Education Research.

Barton, E. E., Chen, C., Pribble, L., Pomes, M., & Kim, Y. (2013). Coaching preservice teachers to teach play skills to children with disabilities. *Teacher Education and Special Education, 36*(4), 330–349.

Barton, E. E., Fuller, E. A., & Schnitz, A. (2016). The use of email to coach preservice early childhood teachers. *Topics in Early Childhood Special Education, 36*(2), 78–90.

Blue Ribbon Panel on Clinical Preparation and Partnerships for Improved Student Learning. (2010). *Transforming teacher education through clinical practice: A national strategy to prepare effective teachers*. Washington, DC: National Council for Accreditation of Teachers Education.

Brauner, C. B., & Stephens, C. B. (2006). Estimating the prevalence of early childhood serious emotional/behavioral disorders: Challenges and recommendations. *Public Health Reports, 121*(3), 303–310.

Caprara, G. V., Barbaranelli, C., Steca, P., & Malone, P. S. (2006). Teachers' self-efficacy beliefs as determinants of job satisfaction and students' academic achievement: A study at the school level. *Journal of School Psychology, 44*(6), 473–490.

Couse, L. J., & Recchia, S. L. (2016). Future directions for early childhood teacher education. In L. J. Couse and S. L. Recchia (Eds.), *Handbook of early childhood teacher education* (pp. 379–387). New York: Routledge.

Gupta, S. S., & Daniels, J. (2012). Coaching and professional development in early childhood classrooms: Current practices and recommendations for the future. *NHSA Dialog, 15*(2), 206–220.

Guskey, T. R. (1982). The effects of change in instructional effectiveness upon the relationship of teacher expectations and study achievement. *Journal of Education Research, 75*(6), 345–349.

Hemmeter, M. L., Hardy, J. K., Schnitz, A. G., Adams, J. M., & Kinder, K. A. (2015). Effects of training and coaching with performance feedback on teachers' use of pyramid model practices. *Topics in Early Childhood Special Education, 35*(3), 144–156.

Horm, D. M., Hyson, M., & Winton, P. J. (2013). Research on early childhood teacher education: Evidence from three domains and recommendations for moving forward. *Journal of Early Childhood Teacher Education, 34*(1), 95–112.

Hustedt, J. T., & Barnett, W. S. (2011). Financing early childhood education programs: State, federal, and local issues. *Educational Policy, 25*(1), 167–192.

Institute of Medicine (IOM) and National Research Council (NRC). (2015). *Transforming the workforce for children birth through age 8: A unifying foundation*. National Academies Press.

Kazdin, A. E. (2011). *Single-case research designs: Methods for clinical and applied settings* (2nd ed.). New York: Oxford University Press.

Knowles, M. S. (1970). *The modern practice of adult education: From pedagogy to andragogy* (Vol. 41). New York: Association Press.

La Paro, K. M., & Pianta, R. C. (2000). Predicting children's competence in the early school years: A meta-analytic review. *Review of Educational Research, 70*(4), 443–484.

National Center on Quality Teaching and Learning (2020, July 13). *Practice-based coaching: Collaborative coaching partnerships.* https://eclkc.ohs.acf.hhs.gov/sites/default/files/pdf/pbc-brief-ccp.pdf

Reinke, W. M., Stormont, M., Herman, K. C., Puri, R., & Goel, N. (2011). Supporting children's mental health in schools: Teacher perceptions of needs, roles, and barriers. *School Psychology Quarterly, 26*(1), 1–13.

Rock, M. L., Schumacker, R. E., Gregg, M., Howard, P. W., Gable, R. A., & Zigmond, N. (2014). How are they now? Longer term effects of e-coaching through online bug-in-ear technology. *Teacher Education and Special Education, 37*(2), 161–181.

Rush, D. D., & Shelden, M. L. L. (2011). *The early childhood coaching handbook*. Baltimore, MD: Brookes Publishing Company.

Ryan, S., & Gibson, M. (2016). Preservice early childhood teacher education. In L. J. Couse and S. L. Recchia (Eds.), *Handbook of early childhood teacher education* (pp. 195–208). New York: Routledge.

Snyder, P. A., Hemmeter, M. L., & Fox, L. (2015). Supporting implementation of evidence-based practices through practice-based coaching. *Topics in Early Childhood Special Education, 35*(3), 133–143.

Sutherland, K. S., Conroy, M. A., Vo, A., & Ladwig, C. (2015). Implementation integrity of practice-based coaching: Preliminary results from the BEST in CLASS efficacy trial. *School Mental Health, 7*(1), 21–33.

Tschannen-Moran, M., & Hoy, A. W. (2001). Teacher efficacy: Capturing an elusive construct. *Teaching and Teacher Education, 17*(7), 783–805.

CHAPTER NINE

Only the Best

Ensuring High-Quality Mentors for Teacher Candidates

Amy Rogers, Gwyneth Price, and John Ziegler

A constant challenge in teacher preparation stems from the need to appropriately match teacher candidates with high-quality mentors during clinical practice. It is not uncommon for teacher candidates to spend numerous hours in clinical practice only to be randomly assigned to a mentor teacher for their clinical internship. Furthermore, institutions maintaining national accreditation (i.e., Council for the Accreditation for Educator Preparation) are faced with the added challenge of meeting standards particularly written with mentor selection in mind. There are no national requirements for qualifications to become a mentor teacher.

However, in Pennsylvania, the requirements include (1) at least three years of satisfactory teaching experience, (2) one year of certified experience in the school where the intern is assigned, (3) certification in the subject competency of the teacher candidate, and (4) being trained by the institution. Many educator preparation programs rely on district and school administrative staff to assist with assigning appropriate clinical practice based on requirements from state departments of education and perhaps standards set forth by professional organizations, such as the Association of Teacher Educators (ATE) and American Association of Colleges for Teacher Education (AACTE).

This chapter outlines best practices for selection of high-quality mentors for teacher candidates. Our research examines (a) criteria used for selection of mentor teachers, (b) processes for determining which teachers qualify to become a mentor teacher, and (c) an analysis of institutional practices that evaluate a mentor teacher. Themes emerging from the study support the need for collaborative partnerships to prepare effective teachers and support our belief in the use of a systematic model for selecting mentor teachers. Common threads from all stakeholders include the selection of mentors who are effective communicators, have consistent classroom management skills, and are willing to share their expertise.

Literature Review

Despite the perceived importance of clinical internships, little research has been conducted to examine factors in the selection of a mentor teacher. As documented in Greenberg et al. (2011), few states have specific guidelines regulating the schools in which student teaching can occur or the teachers that are eligible to supervise mentors.

As a model, coach, and evaluator, the mentor teacher serves a crucial role in helping teacher candidates prepare for transition to effective practice as a beginning teacher. Weiss and Weiss (2001) argued that it is generally accepted by students, teachers, and most faculty members that "cooperating teachers are the most powerful influence on the quality of the student teaching experience and often shape what student teachers learn by the way they mentor" (p. 134). Weiss and Weiss's research supports earlier studies conducted by Marrou (1988) and Zeichner (1980), who also concluded that cooperating teachers have a major influence on the practices of student teachers. Due to the daily role the mentor has with the teacher intern, they are uniquely positioned to influence the student teacher's professional growth.

Research supports the value of the mentor–student teacher relationship as a critical factor to the retention of novice teachers (Clarke et al., 2014) but little around what factors go into the selection of a mentor teacher. In the most recent study by Biggers et al. (2019) results showed that (a) mentor placements are often found through word of mouth versus more formalized systems, (b) there is a wide variety of incentives offered to mentor teachers, and (c) there is a common minimum standard for teachers to qualify as mentor teachers. More so, Biggers et al. (2019) findings supported our claim that further research is needed to determine what factors best support the selection of a mentor teacher.

A centralized system for matching mentor teachers with teacher candidates is necessary to ensure that all parties benefit from the pairing. Cooperating teachers are one of the most influential components of teacher education programs (Blocker & Swetnam, 1995; Grossman et al., 2012).

Many local education agencies' (LEAs) procedures depend heavily on the school administration's selection of a mentor teacher *who is willing* to host a teacher candidate, oftentimes not on *who is qualified* to serve as a mentor nor whether the match between the mentor teacher and teacher candidate is beneficial to either party.

Inarguably, the mentor teacher who guides and supports the candidate throughout the field experience is crucial to the success of the experience (Graham, 2006; Karmos & Jacko, 1977). Yet what qualities are considered essential to be selected as a mentor teacher? Professional organizations, such as the Association of Teacher Educators (ATE) and the American Association for Colleges for Teacher Education (AACTE), support this notion through the development of criteria for selecting mentor teachers to accompany those regulating the selection of clinical practice sites.

The goal is for candidates to merge their conceptual understanding of teaching with the functional knowledge of in-service teachers through a process derived from practice under the guidance of a reflective, experienced practitioner (Harrison et al., 2006). The results from our study confirm the need for clinical partnerships that select only the best mentor teachers who are willing to share their content knowledge, pedagogy, and classroom management skills by utilizing strong communication skills to model and guide the teacher intern.

The clinical internship is the capstone experience for the teacher candidate. It is critical, challenging, and rewarding to all stakeholders and a time of professional growth. As such, teacher candidates need specific guidance from their mentor teachers, who, in turn, should be specifically prepared, trained in supervision, aware of the goals and objectives of the clinical internship, and have holistic knowledge about the teacher education program in which they are participating (Applegate, 1982; Killian & McIntyre, 1987).

Good mentors provide opportunities for the teacher intern to reflect upon and understand teaching (Rowley, 1999) and coaches who provide regular feedback (Farris et al., 1991; McIntyre et al., 1996). Pennsylvania, where our study was conducted, requires the training of mentor teachers as part of the requirements for hosting a teacher intern. Several studies found that mentor teachers with specific training in clinical supervision are better at giving feedback to teacher candidates (Killian & McIntyre, 1987) and improved their communication with teacher candidates (Hauwiller et al., 1988).

In a more pragmatic sense, many educator preparation programs (EPPs) are under the auspices of national accreditation from organizations, such as the Council for the Accreditation of Educator Preparation (CAEP), as well as accountable to statewide reviews. CAEP Standard 2.2 calls for educator preparation programs and PK–12 partners to "co-select, prepare, evaluate, support, and retain high-quality clinical educators" (CAEP, 2015).

Though many model partnerships between universities and PK–12 schools have existed for many years, accountability to state and national reviews now requires evidence of collaboration, cooperation, and mutual evaluation. Producing this evidence is a balancing act for all involved. Maintaining strong relationships while imposing the needs of the university on the PK–12 school environment is a delicate affair, especially if the PK–12 school happens to be unionized and especially due to the omnipresent pressure of accountability through standardized testing. It is within this context that the researchers wanted to not only build a model of best practice for "mentor matching" but to also examine the processes that meet national accreditation standards while maintaining peaceful, productive partnerships.

Systematic Model for Selection of "Only the Best"

Though we dare to posit a "model" for this process, each educator preparation program should use local control and make use of a system that embodies these main principles. They must also meet the needs of their individual program. Based on the collection of data from surveys and interviews, the model we suggest for the selection of only the best mentor teachers include invoking a checklist, such as the following:

1. Develop criteria for selection of schools where clinical internships will occur, including high-poverty, high-functioning schools.
2. Create partnerships with districts where multiple candidates placed in various classrooms can be helpful to all involved. Professional development or training for mentor teachers can be offered to multiple mentors simultaneously on-site, increasing mentor effectiveness.
3. Develop explicit criteria for selection of mentor teachers that ensure that they are not only willing to participate and have the appropriate certifications but also have been evaluated on their communication skills, classroom management techniques, expert content knowledge, and ability to be reflective about their teaching.
4. Share and share alike. Share information up front about selection criteria, processes for matching, technology and paperwork expectations, professional development opportunities, and evaluation procedures.

5. Co-develop the process for gathering data on potential mentors, matching processes, and evaluation instruments.
6. Form an advisory board or similar entity to act as a conduit for idea generation and feedback.
7. Employ a matching process that includes mutual decision-making between the university personnel and school administration.
8. Maintain a cooperative liaison between the university and mentor teachers to provide systematic development of the partnership and assessment of the value of having teacher candidates placed in the schools.
9. Implement evaluation procedures to secure feedback from teacher candidates on mentor teachers, university-based mentors, and LEAs; from mentor teachers on university-based mentors; and from university-based mentors on mentor teachers and placement schools.
10. Finally, for any of this to work, incentivize teachers to become mentors.

Given state requirements, the essential characteristics from literature as well as the results of our surveys and interviews, the model we suggest should be based on matching teacher candidates with high-quality mentors with the following characteristics:

1. A minimum of three years of satisfactory teaching experience.
2. A minimum of one year of certified experience in the school where the intern is assigned.
3. Certification in the subject competency of the teacher candidate.
4. Trained by the institution.
5. Demonstrate a positive impact on student learning and commitment to professional growth.
6. Demonstrate effective communication skills.
7. Willingness to accept the teacher candidate as part of the staff and share school facilities, policies, and procedures.
8. An excellent classroom manager who demonstrates the ability to engage students in the learning environment.
9. A true professional who is a reflective practitioner and is willing to evaluate the performance of the student teacher.
10. A mentor who is willing to support and direct a student teacher's professional development.

Methodology/Results

Survey Design and Procedure

Before designing the model, we started by acknowledging the following realities: (1) each educator preparation program uses its own system of selecting mentor teachers, (2) certain characteristics are more desirable for choosing mentors, and (3) mentors are often selected based solely on availability for the upcoming year. Given these assumptions, we set out to determine how each group of stakeholders perceived the characteristics of accomplished mentors for selection and what processes they would be open to in making the best possible match between mentor and mentee.

To do this, we began by surveying three major stakeholder groups involved in the selection and matching process. Such stakeholders included the school district administrators, the university personnel in charge of placing the candidates, and the teachers who agree to participate as mentors. Follow-up data was collected via a structured interview process of selected representatives from the same stakeholder groups. In the end, our study used a mix of quantitative and qualitative data to examine the following questions:

1. What criteria are used for selection of mentor teachers?
2. What are the processes for determining which teachers qualify as a mentor teacher?
3. What institutional practices appropriately address the evaluation of a mentor teacher?

Data Collection and Analysis

Our research began in 2016 when the researchers sent surveys to over 800 administrators, 10,000 teachers, and over 100 university-based field placement coordinators. These numbers reflect the use of convenience sampling and used publicly available contact information through particular databases held by the institutions. The survey collected quantitative data on each of our research questions and was considered phase 1 of the research study. Phase 2 employed a qualitative approach using interview questions with individuals representing the same three stakeholder groups. Participants in the interviews were not necessarily survey participants but were selected specifically to stratify across stakeholder groups as well as sample a diversity of institutions, including rural/suburban/urban school district and institution size. The conversations were transcribed, coded, and then analyzed to gain parallel information to the survey data. These data were considered together to enrich answers to our research questions.

Q1—Criteria for mentor selection. For question one, a list of criteria associated with mentors was developed through a synthesis of the literature. Participants were asked to rank the criteria, with a number 1 ranking being the most important. Survey response rates reflected participation by 6% administrators, 2.5% to 3% teachers, and 30% university-based teacher educators. Raw scores and individual rankings were averaged for each group and then divided into categories of "top 5," "next 5," and "bottom 5." Those results are shown in table 9.1.

Table 9.1. Criteria for High-Quality Mentors

Criteria for High-Quality Mentors	Survey Administrators	Survey Teachers	Survey Field Directors	Interview Participants
Content area/grade level	next 5	next 5	top 5	next 5
Availability/willingness to participate	next 5	next 5	top 5	next 5
Classroom management skills	next 5	next 5	next 5	next 5
Good communication skills	next 5	next 5	next 5	next 5
Values relationships	next 5	next 5	next 5	bottom 5
Willingness to share expertise	next 5	next 5	top 5	next 5
Empathy/cultural responsiveness	next 5	top 5	next 5	bottom 5
Forward thinking/progressive	next 5	next 5	next 5	bottom 5
Commitment to the profession	next 5	next 5	next 5	next 5
Expert content knowledge	next 5	next 5	top 5	next 5
Reflective	bottom 5	bottom 5	next 5	next 5
Technology skills	bottom 5	bottom 5	next 5	bottom 5
Knowledge of policies, procedures, and laws	bottom 5	bottom 5	next 5	next 5
Patience	bottom 5	next 5	next 5	bottom 5
Mentor Experience	bottom 5	bottom 5	bottom 5	next 5

Note: ● = top 5   ◐ = next 5   ● = bottom 5

When looking at a single criterion, there was no criterion that all stakeholder groups could agree on as being the most important. Valuing relationships, forward thinking/progressive, and commitment to the profession were each thought of highly but did not rise to the top for many. Mentor experience was not considered vital as a characteristic by any group and, interestingly, neither was expert content knowledge. What can be seen, however, are the similarities between administrators and teachers, which were observed in the interview group as juxtaposed with differing answers of the university field directors.

The reason probably comes down to "practicality." Administrators and teachers when answering this question were most likely practical in stating that, without the right content area or grade level or the willingness to participate, there would be no successful placement. For much the same reason, the university field directors may not worry about that characteristic and pass over it when completing their rankings because, without those two pieces, the mentor would not even be on the list to consider.

> It is not a choice with content and availability. I look for a teacher that has both. Teachers who supervise and mentor teacher candidates are recognized as the emerging teacher leaders in our schools. But I need someone who is willing to participate.

Striking differences can be observed with criteria such as technology skills and knowledge of policies between university personnel and personnel from LEAs. These differences most likely stem from the reality that most paperwork and assessments are now completed electronically and online platforms are used to collect data by many universities, making technology usage an important factor. Similarly, with the focus of universities on ensuring the proper certification of candidates and the need to avoid liabilities for the uncertified teacher candidates, knowledge of policies and laws holds much more importance to the university stakeholders.

It may not be surprising that classroom management was an important criterion for everyone involved in the study. In fact, interviews with mentor teachers revealed this as their top selection. One mentor teacher shared,

> You can learn and study different types of behavioral plans but until you really hit the ground running as a student teacher, being in the classroom all day, using positive reinforcements and procedures, this is where you truly learn to become a full-time teacher. You need a mentor who has strong classroom management skills that can be modeled for the student to practice.

The comment rings true for teacher educators. Students learn theory in methods classes, but the real learning starts when they apply what they know and use this knowledge to best help and serve the needs of the children in their care.

> I had a difficult time in my first year of teaching with managing my students and class. I wish I had a mentor teacher who had stronger management skills and was willing to share tips to help me become more prepared for my own classroom.

Q2—Mentor qualifications. After researching and confirming the criteria that stakeholders involved in the matching process use to determine a "good mentor," it is then a question of how to match those individuals with the mentees who need them. Therefore, in relation to question 2, investigating processes for matching mentors and mentees, the following results were obtained using the same survey and interview participants (see table 9.2). The categories seen in the table were determined by taking the raw ranking data and averaging the responses for PK–12 administrators, university personnel, and PK–12 teachers. Rankings were partitioned or categorized based on the average frequency of response.

As one can clearly observe, the survey confirmed the interview results and demonstrated what researchers knew to be true: current processes are not collaborative in nature and little collaboration occurs between the LEA administrator and the university field director in the matching process. Throughout the qualitative portion of our process, no respondents selected

Table 9.2. Processes for Matching

Processes for Matching	Current	Desired
P–12 school administration provides names of mentors; university assigns mentors to interns.	some/possible	highest
University provides names of interns; P–12 school administration assigns mentors.	some/possible	some/possible
An interview process where the mentor teacher interviews the intern; P–12 school administration decides on the match.	some/possible	highest
An interview process where the mentor teacher interviews the intern; university decides on the match.	none/not willing	highest
A mentor/intern "mixer"—a social gathering to introduce mentors to interns.	none/not willing	some/possible
University and P–12 school personnel meet to make mutual decisions.	none/not willing	some/possible

Note: ● = highest response ◐ = some/possible ● = none/not willing an option that included the university interviews with the mentor, a "mixer" gathering, or a meeting between university and P–12 personnel. Generally, the data shows that current processes are not collaborative in nature and very few institutions involve the teacher candidate in the matching process. What appears even more problematic is that the voice of the mentor teacher is often nonexistent in the matching process. For the most part, administrators ask teachers whether they would be willing to host a student intern but have no collaboration with the matching process. This is evidenced as shared by mentor teachers:

- "I recognized the intern's name when he emailed me because he had been in observing for field experience last year."
- "I would love to be able to request a specific intern, one that I've worked with previously and established a relationship, but that is not how our system runs."

Most current processes are developed to be efficient and straightforward, but do not ensure any match quality. This rather "sterile" process fails to take into account those less practical but still important characteristics, as found in the literature, that influence a beneficial placement. Reflectiveness, commitment, empathy, patience, and progressiveness are all aspects of one's disposition that could invariably make a good or bad match and will have a deep impact on the success of the placement. Whether due to CAEP or for the fulfillment of best practice, universities are trying to expand these processes to be more collaborative and cooperative.

Luckily, the data demonstrates that administrators and teachers are relatively like-minded. Some sort of mutual decision-making process was perceived favorably by both groups. However, it should be noted that, as evidenced by responses to each of the alternatives posed in the survey, administrators across the board would like to maintain a sense of control in the matching process. Beyond mutual decision-making and control, another theme that arose from the interviews was time. The quotes below provide further insight.

Time is an issue, and this is yet another meeting to my schedule.

I would like to work together more and share about our interns, their strengths, and their needs. The LEA administrator knows their teachers and we know our interns. This is by far the best idea, meet and make a mutual decision, yet the time factor does come into play.

Q3—Evaluation of mentor teacher. Co-selection is not the only accreditation-related issue intertwined into the mentor–mentee matching process. There is the effort to try to meet accreditation standards and maintain quality through co-evaluation. This survey produced interesting results. Table 9.3 demonstrates the current processes used by institutions as reported by each of the stakeholder groups.

Table 9.3. Current and Desired Processes for Evaluation of Mentors

Evaluation of Mentors	Current	Desired
Objective instrument completed by university personnel	●	◐
Objective instrument completed by P–12 administration	◐	◐
Survey instrument completed by university personnel	◐	●
Survey instrument completed by P–12 administration	◐	◐
Survey instrument completed by intern	◐	●
Mentor self-evaluation	●	●
Nothing/anecdotal	●	●

Note: ● = frequent/most acceptable   ◐ = some/possible   ● = none/not willing

The form most consistently reported is merely an objective survey instrument completed by the teacher candidate. Though empirical data is important for any university, this form of evaluation may not be the most essential or accurate to determining whether the mentor was effective. Even more concerning, however, is that university personnel report a high rate of "nothing-anecdotal," meaning there seems to be no evidence-based form of evaluation. Both administrators and teachers are open to various forms of evaluation as long as they are objective or survey-like in nature and are completed by a variety of those involved in the relationship.

The overall theme from PK–12 school administrators was that an objective instrument or survey would help the mentor focus and become more reflective. Comments include, "I would support a survey instrument filled out by the intern because we all continue to learn. We like our teachers to be reflective practitioners and an evaluation tool would provide constructive feedback to the mentor." Another administrator shared, "Reflection is valuable for both parties."

Over 50% of university programs shared that their current practice for evaluating the mentor was limited to providing only anecdotal data. An overarching theme was reliance on the university-based mentor to share positives and concerns with fellow university colleagues in an effort to continue to build relationships with the LEAs. When teachers were asked about processes they would support, their answers covered a full range of responses, from not necessary to very valuable. However, 9 out of 20 agreed with use of an objective instrument or survey completed by university personnel. Comments include "I would support an objective instrument or survey as long as I know what I am being evaluated on." Another teacher shared that "she would allow the intern to provide feedback on the experience. This will help us both grow and reflect."

Recommendations

Recognizing the characteristics of an effective mentor teacher can help ensure that teacher candidates are placed in settings that will benefit and support them in their first real teaching endeavor (Glen, 2006). Our data gathered in the form of surveys and interviews suggests that the common thread is *communication* throughout the selection process of matching the teacher candidate to the mentor teacher. Current processes are not collaborative in nature, and very few institutions involve the mentor teacher or the teacher candidate in the matching process. Rather, most current processes are developed to be efficient and straightforward but do not ensure any match quality.

We have created a definitive, collaborative model of co-selection of mentors and candidates and suggest that any model or variation be predicated upon collaborative efforts to improve the quantity, depth, and effectiveness of dialogue between the LEA and the university. The model helps ensure that carefully selected mentor teachers possess the teaching skills and abilities to positively foster professional growth for teacher candidates with whom they work. With a shared mission to prepare teacher candidates, impact student PK–12 student learning, and engage in ongoing professional development, partnerships that span LEAs and university settings are changing the nature of clinical teacher preparation.

Challenges and Opportunities

It is essential that teacher candidates, mentor teachers, and university-based teacher educators function effectively as a team during the clinical internship experience. Each partner within the community of practice has its own goals and needs to meet their respective missions. Therefore, collaboration and communication between the triad of stakeholders sets the stage from the beginning. Careful planning is vital to the process as well as continued support for retention of mentor teachers and clinical partnerships. Good communication is vital to ensuring a positive experience for all involved. A study by Yost (2002) found that teachers who mentored teacher candidates became better communicators, increased their leadership skills, and raised their intrinsic value of their role as a teacher.

To assist the mentors and teacher candidates, it is necessary to support their performance in the classroom from the very beginning of the clinical internship. Support in the form of well-designed and well-maintained clinical partnerships can be pivotal in introducing interns into the profession and keeping them in education. The mentor teacher plays a critical role in improving the professional knowledge and skills that interns need to instruct and prepare students. The college-based educators can provide trainings, offering topics on supervision and feedback to classroom management. Other topics include guiding mentors and interns through the teacher evaluation process in hopes of increasing teacher competence and reducing teacher attrition.

We designed this checklist and subsequent ideas for mentor training from time-tested best practices and our research data. The hope is to provide a systematic model for selection of "only the best" mentors will be used in our home institutions and modified to provide a framework for comparable educator preparation programs. We are excited to share how we meet CAEP standards; sustain effective educator preparation programs; maintain peaceful, productive partnerships with LEAs; and continue to focus on the success of our teacher candidates.

References

Applegate, J. (1982). The impact of construct system development on communication and impression formation in persuasive contexts. *Communication Monographs, 49*(4), 277–289.

Biggers, M., Miller, A., Zangori, L., & Whitworth, B. (2019). (Mis)alignments in mentorship: Exploring challenges to preservice science teacher preparation. *Journal of Science Teacher Education, 30*(4), 344–356.

Blocker, L. & Swetnam, S. (1995). The selection and evaluation of cooperating teachers: A status report. *The Teacher Educator, 30*(3), 19–30.

Clarke, A., Triggs, V., & Nielsen, W. (2014). Mentor teacher participation in teacher education: A review of the literature. *Review of Educational Research, 84*(2), 163–202.

Council for the Accreditation of Education Preparation (CAEP). (2015). Standard 2: Clinical partnerships and practice. http://caepnet.org/standards/standard-2

Farris, P., Henniger, M., & Bischoff, J. (1991). After the wave of reform, the role of early field experiences in elementary teacher education. *Action in Teacher Education*, *13*(2), 20–24.

Glen, W. J. (2006). Model versus mentor: Defining the necessary qualities of the effective cooperating teacher. *Teacher Education Quarterly*, *33*(1), 85–95.

Graham, B. (2006). Conditions for successful field experiences: Perceptions of cooperating teachers. *Teaching and Teacher Education*, *22*(8), 1118–1129.

Greenberg, J., Pomerance, L., & Walsh, K. (2011). Student teaching in the United States. National Council on Teacher Quality. https://www.nctq.org/dmsView/Student_Teaching_United_States_NCTQ_Report

Grossman, P., Ronfeldt, M., & Cohen, J. (2012). The power of setting: The role of field experience in learning to teach. In K. R. Harris, S. Graham, T. Urdan, A. G. Bus, S. Major, & H. L. Swanson (Eds.), *APA educational psychology handbook: Application to learning and teaching* (Vol. 3; pp. 311–334). Washington, DC: American Psychological Association.

Harrison, J., Dymoke, S., & Pell, T. (2006). Mentoring beginning teachers in secondary schools: An analysis of practice. *Teaching and Teacher Education*, *22*(4), 1055–1067.

Hauwiller, J., Abel, F., Ausel, D., & Sparapani, E. (1988). Enhancing the effectiveness of cooperating teachers. *Action in Teacher Education*, *10*(4), 42–46.

Karmos, A., & Jacko, C. (1977). The role of significant others during the student teaching experience. *Journal of Teacher Education*, *28*(5), 51–55.

Killian, J., & McIntyre, J. (1987). The influence of supervisory training for cooperating teachers on preservice teachers' development during early field experiences. *Journal of Educational Research*, *80*(5), 277–282.

Marrou, J. R. (1988–1989). The university supervisor: A new role in a changing workplace. *The Teacher Educator*, *24*(3), 13–20.

McIntyre, D. J., Byrd, D. M., & Foxx, S. M. (1996). Field and laboratory experiences. In J. Sikula, T. J. Buttery, & E. Guyton (Eds.), *Handbook of research on teacher education* (2nd ed.; pp. 171–193). New York: Macmillan.

Rowley, J. (1999). The good mentor. *Educational Leadership*, *56*(8), 20–22.

Weiss, E. M., & Weiss, S. (2001). Doing reflective supervision with student teachers in a professional development school culture. *Reflective Practice*, *2*, 125–154.

Yost, R. (2002). "I think I can": Mentoring as a means of enhancing teacher efficacy. *The Clearing House*, *75*(4), 195–197.

Zeichner, K. M. (1980). Myths and realities: Field-based experience in preservice teacher education. *Journal of Teacher Education*, *31*(6), 45–46.

CHAPTER TEN

Developing Teacher Candidates for the 21st Century

Engaging the Village

Dianne M. Gut-Zippert, Pamela C. Beam,
Heidi Mullins, and Kathleen Haskell

In 2010, the National Council for Accreditation of Teacher Education's (NCATE's) Blue Ribbon Panel called for major changes to how institutions of higher education (IHEs) prepare future teachers. These changes included (a) requiring more rigorous accountability; (b) strengthening candidate selection and placement; (c) revamping curricula, incentives, and staffing; (d) supporting the development and expansion of partnerships; and (e) expanding the knowledge base to identify what works and support continuous improvement (NCATE, 2010).

Faculty and staff of Ohio University's Patton College of Education (PCOE) responded to the call and updated standards outlined by the Association of Teacher Educators (ATE, 2016) for field experiences in teacher education, by transitioning from a traditional model of teacher preparation to a clinically based model of teacher preparation.

NCATE transitioned to the Council for the Accreditation of Educator Preparation (CAEP), and Ohio's PCOE continues to lead by providing a model of clinically based teacher education recognized in the Research-to-Practice Spotlight Series on Clinical Preparation by the American Association of Colleges of Teacher Education.

Effective clinically based teacher preparation programs require commitment from both higher education and preschool through grade 12 (PK–12) school communities. Collaborations allow for a variety of ways to engage. Our collaborations targeted improved communication, mentor development, new leadership roles, and program improvement. In periods of major transition and change, challenges may consist of lack of buy-in, misunderstandings, and turf issues. This chapter illuminates the varied ways our rural college of education engages with the local community to collaboratively develop teacher candidates to positively impact PK–12 student achievement.

Unlike traditional teacher preparation programs, in clinically based teacher preparation, learning through practice is the foundation upon which theoretical knowledge is built (Ball & Cohen, 1999; Ball & Forzani, 2009; Korthagen & Kessels, 1999; Korthagen et al., 2001). The process is clearly articulated by Henning et al. (2018) in their explanation of Cochran-Smith and Lytle's (1999) three domains of knowledge in teacher education (i.e., knowledge-for-practice, knowledge-in-practice, and knowledge-of-practice). They explain:

> In a clinically-based model of teacher education, the practice of teaching (knowledge-in-practice) resides at the core of the program in the form of an extensive series of clinical experiences. Those clinical experiences are enhanced through reflection (knowledge-of-practice), which also is utilized to make connections with the theoretical knowledge (knowledge-for-practice) that informs practice through coursework and professional development programs. Learning in clinically-based teacher preparation programs is grounded in practice, enhanced through reflection, and informed by theory. (Henning et al., 2018, p. 25)

It is our premise that teacher candidates develop skills over time that flourish in an environment melding theory and practice. In response, increased time in the field became the focus of our model of clinical practice. To understand theory at a deep level, teacher candidates must experience theory in practice, and increased time in the field underscored the importance of mentoring and collaboration (Henning et al., 2018). The model and experiences are shared here to inspire and inform others engaged in the development of teacher candidates. Suggestions and examples are offered of ways to enhance clinical practice to positively impact teacher candidate development and increase PK–12 student learning.

Prior to the release of the Blue Ribbon Panel report (NCATE, 2010), the PCOE engaged in an extensive dialogue with community partners, which resulted in an innovative school–university partnership called Communications and Connections (Middleton & Prince, 2011). The focus of this group of individuals from educational institutions in Southern Ohio (IHE faculty and staff, superintendents, and PK–12 faculty) was to enhance communications and connections across the region to improve teacher preparation.

The PCOE's initial self-evaluation process focused on PK–12 partners, and feedback from partner schools was much less positive than anticipated.

Although the PCOE had a long history of partnerships with local schools, it was clear that, with a changing educational landscape, it was even more critical to enhance our partnerships and provide more transparency regarding (a) course and field expectations and (2) accreditation and licensure requirements at the college and state level while giving school partners more voice regarding how to best serve the needs of the PK–12 students of the region.

Design Teams

Another outcome of the self-study was the creation of collaborative committees or work groups, designated as design teams, to serve as communication conduits for all stakeholders. Members of design teams volunteer their time and efforts, and, for university faculty, participation contributes to the service component of their faculty responsibilities. Design teams form the backbone of a fluid model of support and growth and meet at regular intervals throughout the academic year to address issues identified in the self-study and new issues and topics that arise. Initially, three design teams were created; however, additional design teams have been added. The first three design teams are most relevant to this discussion and are described below.

- Design team 1 is made up of area superintendents, principals, classroom teachers, teacher education and educational leadership faculty members and staff who evaluate state-wide initiatives and mandates for PK–12 education and incorporate changes in college program design to reflect those initiatives.
- Design team 2 is made up of area PK–12 building principals and teacher education and educational leadership faculty whose primary role is to evaluate specific building needs and provide recommendations for redesign to support stakeholders within school settings.
- Design team 3 consists of PK–12 teachers, teacher educators, and PCOE administrators who place teacher candidates in school settings for clinical experiences and support PK–12 teachers in their mentoring of PCOE's teacher candidates to facilitate preparation for entering Ohio's four-year teacher residency program designed to support new teachers.

Over the course of the PCOE's transition to a clinically based model of teacher preparation, faculty considered ways teacher candidates could add value to PK–12 classrooms. One way to enhance their contributions was to require teacher candidates to spend more time engaged in PK–12 classrooms. From the outset, as part of their charge, all three design teams were tasked with identifying barriers and solutions to increasing the amount of time candidates spent in the field and enhancing their impact on PK–12 student learning.

Support for Mentor Teachers

Several components were put in place to support mentor teachers in the implementation of a clinically based model of teacher preparation. Two such supports are mentoring modules and the opportunity to earn and utilize college credit waivers.

Gut et al. (2014) used face-to-face interviews with mentor teachers to determine their confidence in mentoring candidates in early field, professional internships, and first-year teachers and identify areas for program improvement. In response to the deficits, members of the teacher education department worked with mentor teachers to develop workshop materials and strategies to support and mentor teacher candidates at all levels of competence.

The initial face-to-face workshop was offered free of charge to all mentor teachers who were supporting teacher candidates. In response to its popularity, members of design team 3 put the workshop online to accommodate participants from across the state. Six additional workshops were developed to support PK–12 mentor teachers (see https://www.ohio.edu/education/clinical-experiences/mentor-teachers).

Recognizing that not all candidates enter with the same knowledge and skills, workshop participants assisted in creating the *Developmental Curriculum for Clinical Experiences in Teacher Education* (Henning et al., 2016). The document reflects the full continuum of teacher development and can be used by mentor teachers working with teacher candidates as well as entry-year or first-year teachers.

Finally, as compensation and recognition of the extensive effort and time mentor teachers spend mentoring and supporting teacher candidates in early field or professional internships (PI), mentor teachers' schools are provided with a reduced-rate tuition waiver each time a mentor teacher hosts a professional intern. Each PK–12 school develops its own criteria for determining eligibility and awarding of waivers to interested mentor teachers.

Support for Teacher Candidates

In the PCOE, a range of individuals and structures have been put into place to assist and support teacher candidates during their teacher preparation program.

OHIO Center for Clinical Practice in Education (OHIO CCPE)
The main purpose of the OHIO CCPE is to foster and support outreach activities that connect the PCOE with PK–12 schools. Existing partnerships are with seven school districts and 12 buildings at the elementary, junior high, and high school levels in the local area and one new urban partnership, which expands opportunities available to teacher candidates.

Office of Clinical Experiences
Staff in the Office of Clinical Experiences engage with PK–12 school partners to collaboratively "place teacher candidates in educational settings that benefit all stakeholders through supported partnerships" (Ohio University, 2019). Partners in our model of teacher preparation include school-based teacher educators whose role is to supervise, support, and assess teacher candidates during the professional internship experience.

Systems That Support Replication

Extended Time
The initial focus of the PCOE's transition to a clinically based teacher preparation program was to increase the amount of engaged time teacher candidates spent in the field. The PCOE had a history of partnerships at the early childhood education (ECE) level with extended field experiences facilitated through the OHIO CCPE. The ECE junior field experience has candidates spending two full days a week in their field placement for nearly a full academic year. This extended field time is possible since ECE candidates take all junior and senior coursework in the PCOE, as opposed to other programs that may require coursework outside of the PCOE.

Using the ECE partnerships as a model and in collaboration with our PK–12 partners, the PCOE faculty incrementally increased the time other licensure candidates spent in the field. One challenge unique to the middle-childhood education (MCE) licensure, Multi-Age, Modern Languages, and Adolescent to Young Adult education (AYA; i.e., secondary) licensure areas was associated with having to schedule around content courses teacher candidates take in other colleges outside the PCOE (i.e., Arts and Sciences, Fine Arts).

In one case, a middle childhood partnership was developed where candidates were assigned to the same classroom for most of the school year, spending 80 hours in the classroom each semester.

To accommodate majors with significant coursework outside of the PCOE taken during the junior year, the amount of time candidates spent in the professional internship/student teaching experience during the senior year was increased. In this revised model, the senior year was divided into Professional Internship 1 (PI1) and Professional Internship 2 (PI2), which ideally allow teacher candidates to spend a full year in the same classroom to enhance their ability to positively impact PK–12 student learning.

The PI1 and PI2 occur during candidates' senior year with expectations aligned to the Ohio Standards for the Teaching Profession. As a result, candidates are poised to move directly into a teaching position after completing their internships, where they will begin the four-year residency program in the State of Ohio.

To support the internships, there are four large college-wide seminars that focus on clinical expectations for PI1 and PI2, the Educational Teacher Performance Assessment (edTPA) and the Resident Educator Summative Assessment (RESA), Alice Training, and Trauma Informed Practice. Additional topics addressed during small group seminars are left up to the discretion of school-based teacher educators and target specific needs and concerns of the teacher candidates in that group. Figure 10.1 provides a visual representation of program components.

Figure 10.1. Components of Support Provided in the Patton College of Education's model of clinical practice

Disposition and Credential Review

One concern associated with increased time in the field was for teacher candidates who might be struggling, who are not a good fit for the classroom or not a good match for the assigned mentor teacher. Revisions were made to the PCOE disposition review process (all candidates are evaluated at three transition points), and an exit strategy was articulated. An intervention disposition review process was also developed for use in cases where candidates might be struggling. One possible outcome for individuals referred for professional disposition interventions is the development and implementation of an improvement plan, which is a remediation plan developed for and agreed to by teacher candidates needing extra support to successfully complete their program of study.

Outcome Measures of Candidate Success

To measure the quality of programming provided by the PCOE, teacher candidate outcomes are assessed using a variety of instruments. Formal, valid, and reliable assessments used to evaluate teacher candidate outcomes include the Candidate Preservice Assessment of Student Teaching (CPAST), the Ohio Assessments for Educators (OAE), and the Educational Teacher Performance Assessment (edTPA), all of which are described here.

Created by a collaborative of 26 educator preparation programs (EPPs) in the State of Ohio under the leadership of researchers at the Ohio State University, the CPAST assesses teacher candidate performance. The CPAST, which is copyrighted, assesses two major areas of pedagogy and dispositions and comprises seven major categories: planning for instruction and assessment, instructional delivery, assessment, analysis of teaching, professional commitment and behaviors, professional relationships, and critical thinking and reflective practice.

These seven categories are further divided into specific elements of practice. A rubric containing item descriptors, sources of evidence, and possible evidence guides scoring of teacher candidate performance. Elements are scored on a 3-point scale (3 = exceeds expectations, 2 = meets expectations, 1 = emerging, or 0 = does not meet). The assessment is completed individually by the teacher candidate, school-based teacher educator, and mentor teacher, followed by a meeting to discuss and determine an agreed upon "consensus" score.

Since the CPAST was adopted for use in the 2015–2016 academic year, no scores are available prior to the implementation of our clinically based programming for comparison purposes. However, over the three years reported, mean scores on the CPAST for teacher candidates ranged from a low of 29.55 in 2015–2016, to a high of 33.54 in the academic year 2018–2019. Individual scores ranged from a low of 13 to a high of 58. See table 10.1.

Table 10.1. Candidate Preservice Assessment of Student Teaching Form (CPAST) Final Consensus Pedagogy Score by Semester/Year

Semester/Year	n	Mean	Range Minimum	Maximum
2015–2016	296	29.75	13	58
2017–2018	356	32.60	13	39
2018–2019	294	33.54	13	39

Note: Highest possible score = 63. Only final consensus pedagogy scores are reported here.

The OAE is a licensure exam required for licensure in the State of Ohio. Created by Pearson's Evaluation Systems, the OAE measures professional, pedagogical, and subject-specific knowledge and skills. All teacher candidates seeking initial licensure must take a pedagogy assessment of professional knowledge, which is grade-level band specific (i.e., early childhood, middle childhood, adolescent to young adult, multi-age). Scaled scores are reported that range from 100 to 300, with a passing cut score of 220 set by the State of Ohio. Score reporting is delayed one year, so 2017–2018 is the most recent academic year for which scores are available.

Prior to the implementation of our clinically based model of teacher preparation (2013–2014), the mean score for the OAE across 296 candidates was 245.38 with individual scores ranging from 167 to 288 and a pass rate of 86%. Since the implementation of a clinically based model of teacher preparation, over the most recent three-year period, teacher candidates at our university earned mean scores ranging from a low of 245.75 in 2015–2016 to a high of 259.27 in 2017–2018. Individual scores ranged from a low of 121, to a high of 297. Pass rates were consistently at or above 90%. See table 10.2 for a summary of OAE scores by year.

The edTPA, developed by faculty and staff at the Stanford Center for Assessment, Learning, and Equity (SCALE), is a performance-based, subject-specific assessment and support system used to emphasize, measure, and support the skills and knowledge needed by all teachers (about edTPA, https://www.edtpa.com/). The PCOE assesses teacher candidates' performance on three tasks: planning, instruction, and assessment. Teacher candidates prepare a portfolio and videos demonstrating readiness to teach with lessons designed to support students' strengths and needs, engage students in learning,

Table 10.2. Ohio Assessments for Educators (OAE) Assessment of Professional Knowledge Scores by Year

Year	n	Mean	Range Minimum	Range Maximum	Pass Rate
2015–2016	233	245.75	191	282	94%
2017–2018	343	250.36	121	297	95%
2018–2019	384	259.27	159	278	90%

Note: Passing score = 220. Only Assessment of Professional Knowledge scores presented here.

analyze student learning, and adjust instruction. IHEs select their own levels of mastery, and, for the PCOE, passing scores range from 30 to 43 with any score <30 being a failing score.

In 2013–2014, which was prior to our implementation of a clinically based model of teacher preparation, 441 teacher candidates earned a mean score of 38.47, with scores ranging from 11 to 45 and an 84% pass rate. During the 2014–2015 academic year, 363 candidates had a mean score of 41.92, ranging between 11 and 61 and a 95% pass rate. Since the implementation of a clinically based model of teacher preparation, teacher candidates earned mean scores ranging from a low of 41.95 in 2017–2018, to a high of 42.97 in 2016–2017. Over the three years, individual scores ranged from a low of 25 to a high of 65. The yearly pass rate was consistently 95% or greater. See table 10.3 for edTPA scores by year.

Table 10.3. Education Teacher Performance Assessment (edTPA) Scores by Year

Semester/Year	n	Mean	Range Minimum	Range Maximum	Pass Rate
2016–2017	371	42.97	25	58	96%
2017–2018	352	41.95	29	60	95%
2018–2019	324	42.01	20	65	95%

Note: Institutional cut score = 31–30; ≥43–30 acceptable.

Conclusion

Our purpose for transitioning to a clinically based model of teacher preparation was to give teacher candidates extended time in the field, with the intended outcome of improvements in candidate skills and P–12 student learning. Results indicate the PCOE's transition to a clinically based model of teacher preparation resulted in candidates who continued to meet or exceed scores on pedagogy-related assessments.

Our traditional model was characterized by a lack of communication that often led to misunderstandings, confusion, and frustration (Gut et al., 2014), which resulted in many PK–12 classroom doors being closed. In some districts, high-stakes testing results made up a large part of teachers' annual evaluations with implications for merit-based raises and teacher effectiveness. Understandably, teachers expressed concern that hosting teacher candidates was an added risk to their students' progress on high-stakes assessments.

After the transition, increased collaboration and communication between university and PK–12 educators regarding changes in expectations for teacher candidates and the intended impact on PK–12 student learning was instrumental in reversing this trend, allowing access to more classrooms than were previously available.

Partnerships and increased collaboration between university-based teacher educators, school-based teacher educators, and mentor teachers were critical to the success our teacher candidates and their PK–12 students are now experiencing. Through the ongoing utilization of communication and support structures, mutually beneficial and collaborative partnerships, and supports put in place by faculty, staff, and administrators of the PCOE, teacher candidates and PK–12 students learn together and reap the enhanced benefits.

References

Association of Teacher Educators (ATE). (2016). *Standards for field experiences in teacher education.* Fairfax, VA: Author. https://ate1.org/resources/Documents/Standards/Revised%20ATE%20Field%20Experience%20StandardsII.pdf

Ball, D. L., & Cohen, D. K. (1999). Developing practice, developing practitioners: Toward a practice-based theory of professional education. In L. Darling-Hammond & G. Sykes (Eds.), *Teaching as the learning profession: Handbook of policy and practice* (pp. 3–32). San Francisco: Jossey-Bass.

Ball, D. L., & Forzani, F. (2009). The work of teaching and the challenge for teacher education. *Journal of Teacher Education, 60*(5), 497–511.

Cochran-Smith, M., & Lytle, S. L. (1999). Relationships of knowledge and practice: Teacher learning in communities. *Review of Research in Education, 24*(1), 249–305.

Gut, D. M., Beam, P. C., Henning, J. E., Cochran, D., & Knight, R. (2014). Teachers' perceptions of their roles as a mentor in three different contexts: Early field experiences, student teaching, and entry year teaching. *Mentoring and Tutoring: Partnerships in Learning, 22*(3), 240–263.

Henning, J. E., Erb, D. J., Randles, H. S., Fults, N., & Webb, K. (2016). Designing a curriculum for clinical experiences. *Issues in Teacher Education, 25*(1), 23–38.

Henning, J. E., Gut, D. M., & Beam, P. C. (2018). *Building mentoring capacity in teacher education.* New York: Routledge.

Korthagen, F. A. J., & Kessels, J. P. A. M. (1999). Linking theory and practice: Changing the pedagogy of teacher education. *Educational Researcher*, 28(4), 4–17.

Korthagen, F. A. J., Kessels, J., Koster, B., Lagerwerf, B., & Wubbels, T. (2001). *Linking practice and theory: The pedagogy of realistic teacher education.* Mahwah, NJ: Lawrence Erlbaum Associates.

Middleton, R. A., & Prince, B. L. (2011). Redesigning teacher education from the ground up: A collaborative model. In G. Wan & D. M. Gut (Eds.), *Bringing schools into the 21st century* (pp. 225–246). New York: Springer.

National Council for Accreditation of Teacher Education (NCATE). (2010). *Transforming teacher education through clinical practice: A national strategy to prepare effective teachers.* http://caepnet.org/~/media/Files/caep/accreditation-resources/blue-ribbon-panel.pdf

Ohio University. (2019). Clinical experiences. https://www.ohio.edu/education/clinical-experiences

About the Editors

Dr. Philip E. Bernhardt is currently a professor of secondary education and associate director of the honors program at the Metropolitan State University of Denver. Dr. Bernhardt has spent two decades working in public schools, including eight years as a secondary social studies teacher. He frequently presents on topics that include barriers to higher education; co-teaching; academic tracking; teacher professional development; curriculum design and assessment; and teacher preparation, induction, and mentoring. Dr. Bernhardt has published numerous journal articles and book chapters, and he recently co-published *Digital Citizenship: Promoting Wellness for Thriving in a Connected World*, a textbook designed to support middle and high school students' understanding of their digital footprint and the unintended consequences associated with habitual use of the internet and social media. Dr. Bernhardt earned his MAT in social studies education from Boston University and received his doctorate in curriculum and instruction from the George Washington University.

About the Editors

Dr. Thomas R. Conway is currently chairperson of teacher education and assistant director of the honors program at Cabrini University in Radnor, Pennsylvania. Dr. Conway spent 19 years teaching and administrating at the high school level before moving full-time to higher education. Dr. Conway has worked on several Pennsylvania grants that have researched the use of instructional coaching and mentoring during the student teaching/clinical internship time frame of teacher preparation. In addition to this grant work, Dr. Conway has also worked on grants that have focused on early intervention strategies and mentoring within the early childhood context. Dr. Conway has presented on the topics of mentoring/coaching, secondary education, and early childhood at a variety of state, national, and international conferences. Dr. Conway earned his BA in secondary education/social studies, MA in theological and pastoral studies, and EdD in educational leadership from Saint Joseph's University.

Dr. Greer M. Richardson is currently the director of graduate programs and associate professor of education at La Salle University in Philadelphia, Pennsylvania. Dr. Richardson is also the associate director of the Philadelphia Regional Noyce Partnership, a collaborative of regional higher education institutions dedicated to supporting the STEM teacher pipeline. In recent years, Dr. Richardson has also led two instructional coaching grant initiatives supporting the development of teacher leaders as well as early learning school principals. Dr. Richardson has presented extensively on teacher mentoring, new teacher induction, instructional coaching, and collaborative partnerships at state, national, and international conferences. Her most recent co-publication, titled "Using Instructional Coaching to Support Student Teacher–Cooperating Teacher Relationships," highlights the efficacy of instructional coaching to improve the teacher candidate–mentor teacher relationships. Dr. Richardson earned her MEd from Rutgers University and her PhD from Temple University, both in educational psychology.

About the Contributors

Caroline Powders-Forrest has worked in the field of education for the past 25 years as an elementary and reading intervention teacher. She earned her MEd at the University of Illinois, specializing in reading instruction. For the past eight years, she has served as a clinical coach and lecturer at Western Colorado University, guiding teacher candidates through their residency year as they integrate content and pedagogy courses with their clinical experience.

George Kamberelis is professor, chair, and graduate program director in the Department of Education at Western Colorado University. He earned his PhD in education and psychology from the University of Michigan. Most of Professor Kamberelis' teaching and research has focused on literacy education; classroom talk and social interaction; and qualitative research methods.

Ian Parker Renga is associate professor of education at Western Colorado University in Gunnison, Colorado. A former middle school math, science, and fine arts teacher, he coordinates Western's MEd capstone experience and teaches courses in educational foundations, action research, and instructional methods. His recent research examines the intersection of desire and narrative in teacher education.

Alissa Tower taught in public schools in Colorado and Louisiana for ten years before becoming the director of Educator Licensing at Western Colorado University. She earned her JD at University of Denver as a Chancellor

Scholar focusing on public interest law and her MEd at Columbia University's Teachers College, specializing in school leadership.

Cori Woytek has worked in the field of education for the past 16 years as an elementary teacher and university lecturer. She earned her MS in reading from Gwynedd-Mercy University. For the past ten years, she has served as a lead clinical coach and lecturer in the Education Department at Western Colorado University.

Allison R. Magagnosc is a social scientist who has completed over a dozen research and evaluation studies of pre-service and in-service teacher professional development initiatives. She earned her BA in sociology and an elementary education teacher certificate from Gettysburg College, and her MS in statistics, measurement, assessment, and research technology from the University of Pennsylvania.

Ingrid T. Everett has taught mostly early childhood education courses for the past six years in the Teaching and Learning Department at Bloomsburg University. She also managed a Pennsylvania Department of Education grant at the university and is completing her doctoral studies on culturally responsive teacher self-efficacy in early childhood teacher preparation. Her interests include social justice and equity in education.

Deborah Yost is professor emeritus of education at La Salle University. She has published widely on topics related to instructional coaching, writing engagement in urban schools, reflection, and classroom management. She is the architect of the instructional coaching model chronicled in this chapter. She holds both a MA and PhD in special education from the University of Connecticut.

Greer M. Richardson is the director of graduate programs and associate professor of education at La Salle University. She has presented extensively on teacher mentoring, new teacher induction, instructional coaching, and collaborative partnerships at state, national, and international conferences. She earned her MEd from Rutgers University and her PhD from Temple University, both in educational psychology.

Thomas R. Conway is chairperson of teacher education at Cabrini University. He is also a board member for the Pennsylvania Association of Colleges and Teacher Educators. He has worked on several grants that have included a goal of providing training for mentor teachers and teacher leaders on topics such as instructional coaching and professional learning communities. He earned his MA in theological and pastoral studies and an EdD in educational leadership from Saint Joseph's University.

Allison R. Magagnosc is a social scientist who has completed over a dozen research and evaluation studies of pre-service and in-service teacher professional development initiatives. She earned her BA in sociology and an elementary education teacher certificate from Gettysburg College, and her MS in statistics, measurement, assessment, and research technology from the University of Pennsylvania.

Alana M. Mellor is a high school social studies teacher. She has over 15 years of experience in education, working as a K–12 teacher, a grant program administrator, a student teaching supervisor, and an adjunct instructor. She earned her Bachelor of Arts in political science from the University of Rochester and an MSEd from the University of Pennsylvania, where she received her certification in secondary social studies and a certificate in online instruction.

Glenda L. Black is an associate professor at the Schulich School of Education, Nipissing University. She has worked in the Canadian school system for more than 20 years as a teacher, administrator, and teacher educator. Awarded numerous federal and provincial grants, Glenda has researched and written extensively on teacher education. Her areas of interest are Indigenous education, international teaching, curriculum development, and action research.

Anna-Liisa Mottonen, an assistant professor, teaches for the child and family studies and psychology programs as a sessional instructor at Nipissing University. She has considerable experience teaching in the areas of statistics and research methods, as well as developmental psychology. Anna-Liisa's past research has focused on the development of children's reading skills, self-directed learning, and teacher education.

Amy R. Guenther is an assistant professor in the Office of Medical Education Research and Development at Michigan State University where she develops and facilitates professional learning on effective teaching practices. Dr. Guenther's research focuses on teacher learning, mentoring, and teaching in field settings.

Lindsay J. Wexler is an assistant professor of education at North Central College in Naperville, Illinois. She centers her work around novice teacher learning. Dr. Wexler's research focuses on ways to support novice educators during student teaching and the induction years, specifically looking at the role of mentoring in the learning to teach process.

Susan K. Brondyk is the Irwin B. and Margie E. Floyd Endowed Associate Professor of Education at Hope College where she teaches undergraduate preservice teachers and co-coordinates professional learning opportunities for the program's mentors. Dr. Brondyk's research examines mentor preparation at both the pre-service and induction levels.

Randi N. Stanulis, professor and assistant dean for professional development in the College of Human Medicine, leads educator development on effective teaching and learning practices. Formerly a professor in the College of Education at Michigan State University for 18 years, Dr. Stanulis led initiatives to support mentor and beginning teacher ambitious teaching with a focus on work in urban settings.

Stacey Pylman is an assistant professor in the Office of Medical Education Research and Development at Michigan State University College of Human Medicine in East Lansing, MI. Her research interests include mentoring, instructional coaching, active learning, and clinician-educator teacher identity development.

Romena M. Garrett Holbert is an associate professor of teacher education at Wright State University where she teaches courses in foundations of education, assessment, and research. Building classroom community and effectively responding to needs emergent from diverse life experiences focus her work.

Amy E. Elston is a lecturer and assistant director in the Offices of Partnerships and Field Experiences at Wright State University. Making connections with, organizing learning opportunities for, and showing appreciation of educators is the focus of her work.

Tracey A. Kramer is a senior lecturer and director of Partnerships and Field Experiences at Wright State University. She has been involved with P–16 education for 25 years, with a particular focus on teacher candidate preparation.

Brooke K. Langan currently serves as the assistant dean in the College of Education at East Stroudsburg University of Pennsylvania. In her previous role as director of Field Experiences and Partnerships, Brooke focused her research in the areas of educator preparation, training mentor teachers, and online learning. Upon entering her first role in higher education, training mentors arose as a professional challenge which negated the development of the online platform for the training of mentor teachers. This focus guided Brooke through her doctoral studies and has resulted in an ongoing presentation series for the Pennsylvania Association of Colleges and Teacher Educators from 2017 to 2020. In her new role as assistant dean, Dr. Langan is eager to expand her research portfolio to tackle future projects in online accessibility and enhancing engagement online for teacher candidates and clinical coaches alike.

Kathleen L. Post has been at East Stroudsburg University for the past five years as the Teacher Education Unit Assessment and Accreditation specialist and Tk20 Unit Administrator. In this role, Kathy implemented and managed the College of Education assessment infrastructure in preparation for CAEP accreditation and PDE Major Review. In collaboration with the director of Field Experience and Partnerships, Kathy was part of the design of the online mentor teacher training course in Canvas. Kathy brings vast experience to her role at the university, which includes teaching 7th to 12th grade mathematics and computers as well as designing interactive math lessons for an online learning management system. As a 2020 graduate of the educational leadership and administration doctoral program at East Stroudsburg University, Kathy examined how targeted online learner analytics impacted the digital pedagogy of preservice teacher candidates, which combined research interest in teacher education with instructional technology, online learning, and data literacy.

Toni Miguel is a consultant with Early Intervention Technical Assistance in the Pennsylvania Training and Technical Assistance Network. Her work focuses on supporting early childhood personnel to deliver high quality, inclusive, and equitable educational experiences for diverse young children. She is a recent graduate of the University of North Carolina at Chapel Hill where she conducted research on coaching, social-emotional development, and effective teacher education methods.

John Ziegler is a faculty member in the Middle & Secondary Education and Educational Leadership Department at Edinboro University of Pennsylvania.

Dr. Ziegler has a DEd in administration and leadership studies from Indiana University of Pennsylvania and master degrees in school administration and supervision from St. Bonaventure University and in school guidance and counseling from West Chester University. Dr. Ziegler has held numerous positions from teacher to counselor to school administrator K–12 and now teaches pre-service and graduate courses specifically designed for candidates seeking instructional and school administrative certification. Dr. Ziegler's 45 years of experience in public education define a professional career that serves students and colleagues with distinction. His educational role characterizes a facilitator, a motivator, and a resource who can move individuals from their comfort zones to higher levels of academic and personal growth.

Gwyneth Price is the dean of the College of Education, Health and Human Services at Clarion University of Pennsylvania. She has spent over 25 years in public education as both a high school science teacher, education professor, and administrator. Throughout that time, she has maintained a focus on field experiences first as a mentor, then a supervisor, accreditation coordinator, and now unit head and facilitator of unique field experiences such as residency programs. With a bachelor's degree and certification in chemistry from Bucknell University, as well as a master's and PhD in educational psychology from Pennsylvania State University, Gwen's main objective has always been to understand how to capitalize on experiences to improve student learning.

Amy Rogers is an associate professor and chair of the Education Department at Lycoming College, Williamsport, Pennsylvania. She has over 25 years' experience in public education as a social studies teacher, literacy coach, and professor of education. Amy holds degrees from Lycoming College, Bloomsburg University, and earned her PhD at Pennsylvania State University. Amy is active in the education profession with her work as a member of the Association of Teacher Educator (ATE) National Task member, board member of the Pennsylvania Association of Colleges and Teacher Educators (PAC-TE), a member of the PA Deans of Education Forum, and a program reviewer for the Pennsylvania Department of Education. She served as co-chair for Lycoming College's Middle States Accreditation and Chief Certification and Accreditation Officer.

Dianne M. Gut-Zippert is a professor of special education in the Patton College of Education at Ohio University. She received her PhD from the University of North Carolina at Chapel Hill and teaches graduate and undergraduate courses in special education and curriculum and instruction. Her major research interests include mentoring, interventions for students with disabilities, and integrating twenty-first century skills into the curriculum.

Pamela C. Beam recently retired as a senior lecturer in curriculum and instruction and secondary education courses in the Patton College of Education at Ohio University. She received her PhD from Ohio University in curriculum and instruction and currently teaches graduate and undergraduate courses as an adjunct instructor. Her research agenda encompasses mentoring at multiple levels, and the re-visioning of the clinical model.

Heidi Mullins served as the director of the Office of Clinical Placements as an adjunct instructor for the Patton College of Education at Ohio University. She received her MEd in education from Marygrove College and her BS in elementary education. She has extensive experience as a teacher liaison for a Professional Development School and as an elementary teacher.

Kathleen Haskell is the coordinator of professional internships in the Patton College of Education at Ohio University. She holds an MEd from Georgetown College in elementary and secondary education. She has extensive experience as a high school teacher and university clinical educator, and in her current role, is responsible for placing well over two hundred professional interns each year.

www.ingramcontent.com/pod-product-compliance
Lightning Source LLC
Chambersburg PA
CBHW030140240426
43672CB00005B/207